CHEESE

The Making of a Wisconsin Tradition

by Jerry Apps
Photography by Steve Apps

Amherst Press
a division of Palmer Publications, Inc.

Amherst, Wisconsin

Published by
Amherst Press
A division of Palmer Publications, Inc.
318 North Main Street
PO Box 296
Amherst, Wisconsin 54406

Library of Congress Cataloging-in-Publication Data

Apps, Jerold W. 1934-
    Cheese, the making of a Wisconsin tradition / by Jerry Apps ;
photographs by Steve Apps, — 1st ed.
        p. cm.
    Includes bibliographical references and index.
    ISBN 0-942495-80-2
    1. Cheese—Wisconsin. 2. Cheese—Wisconsin—History. 3. Cheese
factories—Wisconsin.   I. Title.
SF274.U6A66 1998
641-3'73'09775—dc21   98-12317
                                                               CIP

Printed in the United States of America by
Palmer Publications, Inc.
318 North Main Street
Amherst, Wisconsin 54406

Designed and marketed by
Amherst Press

Dedication

To Wisconsin's first cheese makers,
who started the tradition.

Town Line Cheese Factory (Earl B. Whiting, cheese maker), Gillett, c. 1920.

—From Wisconsin Cheese Makers Association.

Contents

Acknowledgments

I want to thank first the cheese makers and the children of cheese makers who helped me with this project and whose names I have not mentioned here. Without them, this book would have been much less than it is.

Several people deserve special mention. Mike Jones of the Green County Extension Office regularly sent me information about anything cheesy that crossed his desk. He also introduced me to Dr. Bill Hein of the Historic Cheesemaking Center in Monroe. Bill Hein in turn introduced me to the wealth of resources at the center and generously made them available to me. He also accompanied me to area cheese factories and arranged several interviews with cheese makers. John Bussman, an active cheese maker and president of the Historic Cheesemaking Center, was exceedingly helpful in introducing me to the basics of traditional cheese making, especially the making of Swiss cheese. Albert Deppeler, a longtime Green County cheese maker, helped me understand the history of Limburger and Baby Swiss cheeses. Kim Tschudy, New Glarus writer and historian, took me on tours of Green County's back roads, where you find the "real story" of cheese making.

Molly Vanderlin of the Wisconsin Milk Marketing Board provided valuable information about the history of the board and the state's current cheese-making activities. John Oncken, former manager of the American Dairy Association of Wisconsin, shared a brief history of that organization. Don McDowell, former director of the Wisconsin Department of Agriculture, was generous in sharing his recollections of the early days of the Alice in Dairyland program.

Richard Gould, president of the former National Cheese Exchange in Green Bay, searched out the history of that organization for me. John Umhoefer, executive director of the Wisconsin Cheese Makers Association, opened his files to me and made available many interesting historic photos of cheese factories once operating in the state. Neal Jorgensen, dean of the University of Wisconsin-Madison College of Agricultural and Life Sciences, generously shared his thoughts on the history of the dairy industry and its future directions. Professor Norman Olson, former director of the Center for Dairy Research at the University of Wisconsin-Madison, shared the history of that organization.

Mary Jane Hettinga of the Marathon County Historical Society was of great help in providing information about cheese factories in that area. Robert Harker of the Sheboygan County Historical Society and the staff of the Sheboygan County Historical Research Center were generous with their help. John Ebert, director of the Adams House Resource Center, which is operated by the Fond du Lac County Historical Society, shared information about Chester Hazen and the cheese-making industry in that county. Lee Somerville sent me information about historic cheese making in northeast Wisconsin and gave me the background on the cheese factory at Heritage Hill in

Green Bay. James Tanner, director of Stonefield Historic Site, sent me information about the cheese factory there. Clarence Waelchli shared information about the cheese factory at Heritage Park Museum in Shawano.

Several people were helpful in putting me in touch with former cheese makers. These included Walter Helm, Everett Olson, Bea Bretl, Gloria Hafemeister, Connie Halverson, Glenn Lepley, and Karen Reese.

Leo Frigo, formerly with the Frigo Cheese Company, shared with me the history of the Italian cheese company his father founded. Bob Wills of the Cedar Grove cheese factory was generous with his time and facilities—much of the process of how cheese is made today was photographed at his plant.

The developer of the Cheesehead, Ralph Bruno, shared the history of his fast-growing company and helped me understand more about why Wisconsin people run around with huge slices of foam cheese on their heads. T. J. Peterslie, the creator of the Cheddarheads, told me about his highly successful company and the popularity of his Cheddarhead T-shirts, calendars, and other gift items.

Many people read parts of the manuscript, pointing out errors, noting omissions, and spotting tangled use of words. These include John Bussman, Bill Hein, Molly Vanderlin, John Oncken, John Umhoefer, Edward Kerr, Dewey Abram of the Grande Cheese Company, William Schrock of the Salemville Cheese Cooperative, and Norman Olson.

Clarence Olson, former University of Wisconsin dairy specialist, read much of the manuscript and made many useful suggestions. Steve Apps, staff photographer for the *Wisconsin State Journal* and my son, took many of the photographs for the book, and read the entire manuscript. Several times he said "What does this mean?" and changes were made. Terese Allen, food columnist and author, read most of the manuscript and offered many valuable recommendations. My wife, Ruth, listened to the many taped interviews and transcribed them—a tedious, seemingly never-ending job. She also read every word of the manuscript, sometimes two and three times as I wrote and rewrote several of the chapters.

Finally, thanks to the staff of Amherst Press and especially Charles and Roberta Spanbauer. They have believed in and supported my work.

To all of the people I have mentioned and many more, I am indebted.

Jerry Apps

Wayne Center Cheese Factory (F. L. Borchert, cheese maker), Kewaskum, c. 1920.

—From Wisconsin Cheese Makers Association.

1 *The Story of Wisconsin Cheese*

Say cheese and you say Wisconsin. The story of cheese is the story of Wisconsin's dairy heritage. It is a story of farmers, milk cows, dairy barns, and green pastures. It is the story of cheese makers who work their magic and turn milk into cheese.

The story of Wisconsin cheese is also the story of people who wear cheese on their heads—not real cheese but a replica—primarily at football and baseball games as they cheer for the Green Bay Packers and the Milwaukee Brewers. Wisconsin people are often referred to as cheeseheads. Sometimes it is a term of respect. Most of the time (especially when voiced by out-of-staters) it means "a bunch of cheese-loving country bumpkins." Either way, it shows how cheese has taken on a role much larger than food. Cheese has become a symbol for the state of Wisconsin.

Cheese, a seemingly insignificant food made from milk, has made a difference in the lives of thousands of people over several generations. It has provided income for farmers, milk haulers, cheese makers, cheese buyers and graders, wholesalers, and retailers. But the lowly piece of cheese is imbued with much more than economic value. Milking cows and making cheese has been a way of life for thousands of people for more than a hundred years.

Many Kinds of Cheese

Cheese lovers of every stripe, from those who like the mildest of the mild to those who enjoy biting into a smelly piece of

Limburger, will find their favorite cheese is Wisconsin-made. Soft cheese, hard cheese, round cheese, square cheese, cylindrical cheese. White cheese, yellow cheese, white and yellow cheese, cheese flecked with blue, cheese with golden rind, cheese with no rind at all. Cheese with holes in it. Well-known cheese—Swiss, cheddar, Colby, and brick. Cheese not so well-known—Mascarpone, Havarti, Queso blanco, and feta. All are made in Wisconsin.

Wisconsin is clearly the land of cheese—the leading cheese-producing state in the nation, making more than 2 billion pounds a year. California is a distant second, producing less than a billion pounds annually.

More than thirty percent of all the cheese made in the United States comes from Wisconsin. The state leads in the production of cheddar, Colby, and Monterey Jack cheese (together known as American cheese), blue, brick, and muenster cheese. It produces 100 percent of the country's Limburger. In numbers, that equals more than 1 billion pounds of American cheese (most of which is cheddar), 40 million pounds of Swiss cheese (including Gruyère, Sweet Swiss, and Baby Swiss), and more than 800 million pounds of Italian cheese (Asiago, Parmesan, provolone, Romano, and mozzarella) a year.[1]

Wisconsin also produces nearly 95 million pounds of specialty cheeses, such as goat cheese, organic cheese, Ackawi, blue, Brie, Camembert, Edam, feta, Gorgonzola, Gouda, Havarti, Mascarpone, muenster, paneer, and ricotta.

Early Memories

I remember well the day I first set foot in a cheese factory. I was about twelve years old and, as I often had done, rode with my father to the Wild Rose Grist Mill. We hauled cob corn and oats to the mill about every two weeks to have them ground into cattle feed for our milk cows. The cheese factory was located across Highway 22 from the mill, on the banks of the Pine River.

The cheese factory wasn't an especially attractive building, but, like the mill, it was an exciting place for a young farm boy. Milk trucks pulled up regularly to the intake chute, which was what my father called the little door on the side of the building. The milk

---

1. *Wisconsin 1996 Dairy Facts* (Madison, WI: Wisconsin Agricultural Statistics Service, 1996).

Farmer's Central Cheese Factory, Sheboygan County, 1930. Note the farmer, with his team of horses, bringing milk to the factory in a high-wheeled wagon.

—From Sheboygan County Historical Research Center.

hauler, a burly-looking fellow wearing a long canvas apron to protect his clothing, stepped down from the truck's cab and crawled on back of the vehicle where the cans were located. He lifted the cans onto a steel roller apron and pushed them toward the intake door. Before he let go of each can, he loosened the cover with a hammer.

It was an interesting sound, hammer against a filled milk can. Each can contained about ten gallons of milk. The milk cans, with their covers sitting loosely at odd angles, disappeared inside the building. What mysteries went on in there, I wondered? Steam spouted out a pipe on top of the building, more noticeable in winter when it met the cold air. A roaring sound accompanied the burst of steam. Sometimes I wondered if the building was about to blow up, but it never did.

When the milk hauler had finished unloading the milk cans, he drove his truck to the end of the building and began loading empty cans, each one bearing the number of its owner. Our milk cans, which the milk hauler picked up, were numbered 424; someone had painted the numbers with red paint on the top of each can, near the handles, so they could be read easily.

One day, after our grist had been ground and loaded into our pickup truck, Dad said he had to see Marvin Jones, manager of the cheese factory. Would I like to walk over with him? This was my chance to see what went on inside that mysterious building where filled milk cans disappeared and steam gushed from the roof, making an unusual sound.

Upon entering the building, a rush of warm, steamy air hit me full in the face. It was like a summer day inside, except it was the middle of winter and the temperature outside hung around zero. I looked, listened, and smelled. I smelled milk and something more, a smell I hadn't known before. As a farm boy, I had been introduced to many smells, but this was a new one. Similar to the smell of milk, but different, too. Not a bad smell, just a different one. The smell of cheese being made.

I saw several men working around a long, narrow stainless steel vat. They wore white pants, white T-shirts, white caps, and black rubber boots. Everything inside the building was white—the walls, the ceiling, the men's clothing.

One of the workers handed me a chunk of something from one of the vats.

"Here, try this," he said. The chunk was yellowish in color, small, and without any clearly defined shape. I put it in my mouth. It had a squeaky feeling on my teeth, and an interesting taste.

"It's cheese curd," the worker said.

"It's good," I said, after chewing it for a little while. Cheese curd tasted nothing like the "Process" cheese we had been eating at home, and nothing like the cheddar cheese I had eaten at a

Cheese making was often a family project. Here Harry Raisleger, with help from his family, places cheese bandages into cheese hoops prior to pressing. Mutual Dairy Cheese Factory, Kewaunee County, c. 1957.

—From Harry and Lucille Raisleger.

relative's home in Wisconsin Rapids, either. I hadn't liked the cheddar. The taste was much stronger than the mild-tasting cheese to which I had become accustomed.

Dad finished his conversation with Marvin Jones and when we opened the door to leave it was like walking from the Fourth of July into New Year's Day. The crisp, cold winter air struck me. I gasped and shivered a little. I wondered what it would be like to work at a job where every day was summer, and you could eat fresh cheese curds whenever you wanted—not as good as working in an ice-cream plant, I figured, but close.

And so at age twelve I began to realize that cheese isn't just cheese, that it comes in many shapes and has many tastes. My education was just beginning, and I had much to learn.

Although I was growing up on a small dairy farm, I knew little about cheese and cheese making. We didn't eat much cheese at home; I suspect my father thought it was too expensive. About the only time we had "good cheese," as my father called it, was on special occasions such as Christmas or when relatives visited. Good cheese was aged cheddar, as I later learned. We occasionally ate cheese that came in small wooden boxes from the creamery where we sent our milk. I remember the cheese as yellow and mild tasting. My mother called it Process cheese and it was pleasant to eat on a slice of homemade bread.

My next encounter with cheese, beyond eating it with macaroni or as a pizza ingredient, was when I took a food science course at the University of Wisconsin. The Madison campus's Babcock Hall houses a cheese factory and ice-cream plant. I learned about the several different kinds of cheeses made in Wisconsin and how to tell them apart. I also learned how to judge cheese, to tell good cheese from that which is less so. Now, for the first time I learned how to appreciate aged cheddar and a fine Swiss.

My interest in cheese and cheese making continued over the years, especially when I worked, during the late 1950s and early 1960s, as a county extension agent in Green Lake and Brown Counties, where several cheese factories operated. During those years, I saw some little cheese factories becoming larger and many smaller ones closing. The same thing was happening to dairy farms. Smaller farms were going out of business, and those that remained were growing larger. Farmers were milking more cows,

Number of Wisconsin dairy farms:

1929-168,890
1939-160,124
1950-143,000
1960-105,000
1970-64,000
1980-45,000
1990-34,000
1995-28,000

putting up additional silos, adding on to their barns, and buying additional tractors.

These were the years of dramatic change in the rural Midwest. The Wisconsin dairy farmer and the cheese factory were caught in the middle of the stampede to become larger. "Bigger Is Better" was the slogan on nearly everyone's lips, including university agriculture professors, rural bankers, and agricultural agencies. But many farmers and small cheese factory operators weren't so sure about becoming larger. What they did know was they couldn't go on as before. The music sounded the same but the dance had changed. They didn't know the new steps and were tripping over their own feet.

The small, family-run cheese factory is disappearing. Before they—and the cheese makers who once worked in them—died, I wanted to capture their history. Here then is the story of the community cheese factory, from the early days to the present, told by those who worked in the factories and those who depended on them. It's a story of people who committed themselves to milking cows and making cheese, in the best of times and the worst.

Walnut Grove Cheese Factory (Jacob Alder, cheese maker).

—From Historic Cheesemaking Center.

2 *Beginnings*

Several thousand years ago, an Arabian merchant poured some camel's milk into a saddlebag made from the stomach of a young sheep, climbed on his horse, and set out on a long journey across the desert. The day was hot and the traveling difficult. At nightfall, the merchant took out his pouch and discovered the milk had disappeared. In its place were a pale watery liquid and some solid white chunks. He drank the liquid, and although it tasted little like the milk from which it came, it was pleasant. He also tentatively nibbled on the strange, white, irregular chunks in the liquid, and he found they had a delightful flavor.

On that long, hot day, the sun had heated the milk in the saddlebag—the lining of which naturally contained rennet, a milk coagulant that caused curds and whey to form. Thus, the first cheese was made by accident.

This tale cannot be confirmed, but it is the legend that begins the story of cheese. Here are some other early beliefs and facts about cheese:

- Cheese was known to the ancient Sumerians 4,000 years before the birth of Christ.
- Travelers from Asia introduced cheese to Europe.
- Cheese was made in many parts of the Roman Empire, and the Romans introduced cheese making to England. The Romans developed many kinds of cheeses, including soft, salted, and smoked cheeses, and a kind of Limburger. They also experimented with curdling agents other than

rennet—thistle flowers, safflower seeds, and fig bark soaked in water to make extracts that would curdle milk.
- During the Middle Ages, European monks made and improved several varieties of cheeses including muenster.
- Italy emerged as a prominent cheese-making center. Gorgonzola, a type of blue cheese, was made in Italy's Po Valley as early as 879 A.D. In the tenth century, Italy became the focus of cheese making in Europe. Cheese was made in other parts of Europe as well.
- Ancient records from a monastery at Conques, France, mentioned Roquefort cheese in 1070.
- By the time the first explorers came to the United States, much was already known about cheese and cheese making.

Cheese Making in the U.S.

It is not known if Christopher Columbus carried cheese with him in 1492, but the Pilgrims surely did when they arrived in the New World in 1620. The Mayflower's list of supplies included cheese, along with beer.

Home Cheese Making

Before the 1850s, women working in farm kitchens were the cheese makers in the United States. In the early days, women did it all, milking and caring for the cows, as well as making the cheese.

Cheese making involved preparing rennet, which most women disliked as it involved killing a calf and removing its fourth stomach. Rennet was often made a year before it was used. One New York dairy woman claiming thirty years experience favored this method: "To six gallons of water, add salt enough to make a brine sufficient to bear up an egg; scald it and skim it. Then add 12 rennets [calves' stomachs] (having emptied, rinsed, and salted them first), six lemons, and an ounce each of cinnamon cloves."[1]

The cheese-making process most women followed before the 1850s included the following steps:

Strain the milk into a container and adjust the temperature, sometimes by heating the milk directly and often by

---

1. Sally McMurry, *Transforming Rural Life: Dairying Families and Agricultural Change, 1820-1885* (Baltimore, MD: Johns Hopkins Press, 1995), 77.

including milk from recently milked cows. Better-flavored cheese resulted if the cheese maker started with warm milk, about 80 to 90 degrees F. [Without thermometers, women detected ideal temperatures by their sense of touch. Some used their elbows as a thermometer.]

With the milk at the right temperature, add rennet and leave the milk to curdle. This takes about forty minutes to an hour. [The curd was ready when you could just pull your fingers through it.]

When the curd is ready, cut it into small pieces. The curd will sink, with the whey floating above it. At this point, cook the curd. [Cooking time, with temperature between 100 and 140 degrees F., varied from a half-hour to three hours, with the temperature slowly increased. Time and temperature varied from cheese maker to cheese maker and with weather conditions.] After cooking, the curd should squeak when you bite into it.

Drain off the whey, break up the curd and salt it.

Press the curd to remove more whey, and to force the curd into a particular shape. Press from 24 to 48 hours, with the pressure increased gradually.

Remove the cheese from the press, trim it, and oil with whey butter or grease to keep flies away and to promote the formation of a rind.

Cure the cheese, allowing it to ripen and develop its characteristic flavor and texture as enzymes and bacteria transform the protein, fat, and carbohydrates. While curing, turn the cheese frequently, washing and rubbing it in the process—invite men folk to help with this heavy work.[2]

Before 1850, cheese was made by farm women in their kitchens.

On many farms, home cheese making involved much more than making a few pounds of cheese to supply the immediate family. Especially in New York State, kitchen cheese making became an industry. Lack of uniformity among the cheeses that emerged from the home kitchens posed problems in the market-place, however. Aware of this obstacle, some New Yorkers attempted to correct it. Alonzo L. Fish was a champion cheese maker in Herkimer County, New York (apparently when there

2. Ibid., 82-83.

was a competition, the few male cheese makers that were around entered). Fish, working with other cheese makers, tried to define a "prime cheese":

> A prime cheese should be well-made of whole milk. It must be mild rather than strong, melting in the mouth so as to leave "a pleasure-sensation, and a gentle relish for more." It should be free from all taint of whey, have a thin rough rind and, as far as possible, be kept in its original shape. Size was really immaterial; other things being equal, a small cheese could be made quite as well as a large one, size was important "only as far as it may suit the purpose of a particular market."[3]

Tools for home cheese making were crude and heavy. The milk was first heated in brass or iron kettles over a fire, then poured into wooden tubs. Crude wooden knives were used to cut the curd. The presses were primitive and massive. Sometimes the

Emma Ruegsegger scrubbing a thirty-gallon milk can, c. 1912. In some parts of Wisconsin, milk was hauled to the nearby cheese factory in these large cans.

—*From John Bussman.*

---

3. Eric E. Lampard, *The Rise of the Dairy Industry in Wisconsin: A Study in Agricultural Change 1820-1920* (Madison, WI: State Historical Society of Wisconsin, 1963), 64.

cheese maker relied on a heavy stone to do the job. In the 1830s, cheese vats replaced the kettles and tubs. The vats had a two-inch space between the inside and the outside walls, allowing hot water or steam to be used for heating the milk. A removable stopper in the bottom of the vat allowed the whey to drain. The process was somewhat easier with this new equipment, but it was still hard work for women.

In some instances, a cheese room was added to the house, and sometimes even a separate cheese house was constructed. Some were as large as 22 feet by 50 feet, with basements of fieldstones and second floors of wooden construction.[4] But even though these farm-based cheese makers sold their cheese to national and world markets, cheese making was viewed as a home craft, like curing meats and canning vegetables.

Factory Cheese Making

Jesse Williams farmed 265 acres near Rome, New York. He milked sixty five cows, and with his wife Amanda turned out 25,000 pounds of cheese in 1850. When Williams inherited his father's farm, he increased his herd to 160 cows. In 1853, he decided to build a cheese factory to accommodate the milk from his large herd. By 1854, he was receiving milk from ten additional farmers. He called his factory the Rome Cheese Manufacturing Association; it is believed to be the first true cheese factory in the United States.[5]

Some earlier operations had bought homemade curds from local farmers and processed them into cheese. Problems had resulted, however, because it was extremely difficult to combine curds from several sources—the curds usually varied greatly in taste and quality.

But even cheese factories like Williams', which bought milk from farmer patrons, were not immediately accepted. In 1860, many farmers still considered a cheese factory a novelty and said they would never catch on. But catch on they did. By the mid-1870s, community cheese factories were widely distributed in New York State, and home cheese making had essentially disappeared.

Charles Rockwell is credited to have had the first commercial cheese-making operation in Wisconsin. He began making cheese in 1837, near Fort Atkinson. J. G. Pickett began a cheese-making operation near Lake Mills in 1841.

4. McMurry, *Transforming Rural Life*, 82-93.
5. Ibid., 123-124.

With a rich history of cheese making in Europe and in the eastern United States, especially New York, it made sense that both a taste for cheese and the ability to make it would come west with settlers who began pouring into the Midwest in the mid-1800s. But no one could have predicted during these early settlement years that Wisconsin would one day become the major cheese-producing state in the nation.

An unidentified cheese factory with farmers delivering their milk with buggies and wagons, c. 1890. Cheese factories were important social centers in rural communities. Each morning, dairy farmers had the opportunity to talk while they waited to unload their milk.

—From Sheboygan County Historical Research Center.

3 *Wisconsin Cheese Making: 1840-1880*

Dairy farming and cheese making were little known and seldom appreciated in the early years of Wisconsin settlement. French explorer Jean Nicolet set foot in what was to become Wisconsin in 1634, but it would be nearly 200 years before agriculture of any kind took hold in the state.

French fur traders came early to the region, but they were not farmers. Miners from Illinois, who mined lead in southwest Wisconsin beginning in the 1820s, farmed a little, enough to provide food for their families, but for the most part they dug holes.

Then in 1836, Wisconsin became a territory, and settlers began trickling into the state from New England, New York, and Pennsylvania. Some came from Ohio, too, leaving behind worn-out soils or merely seeking their fortunes in a new place. With oxen and horses, sometimes a few sheep and usually a couple of Durham cows trailing behind, they swelled the population of Wisconsin Territory from 11,683 in 1836 to 30,945 in 1840. By 1846 the population had soared to 155,277, and by 1850, after statehood, it had nearly doubled to 305,390.[1]

Soon after the Easterners arrived, other immigrant groups began streaming into the state. The Erie Canal had been completed in 1825, and it was now possible for immigrants to reach Wisconsin via the Great Lakes. Thousands of them did. First came the Germans,

---

1. Alice E. Smith, *The History of Wisconsin: Volume 1, From Exploration to Statehood* (Madison, WI: State Historical Society of Wisconsin, 1973), 466.

followed by Norwegians, Welsh, Irish, Swiss, Dutch, Belgians, Finns, Swedes, Danes, Polish, Italians, Icelanders, and others.

The settlers cleared land, cutting oak and hickory trees and stacking the wood into huge piles for burning. The wind carried the smoke from the burning wood, telling all that great changes were coming. Land that had known only the footfall of the Indian and the French trader was now transformed. Prairie grasses that had undulated in the wind like ocean waves for thousands of years disappeared. Black soil, never before exposed to sunlight, replaced the grasses and trees.

Teams of oxen strained against their yokes as they pulled huge plows that turned the sod. Soon fields of wheat grew on former prairie land. Log buildings appeared—cabins for families and crude barns for oxen and horses. The few dairy cows that farmers owned were largely ignored, milked by the farmers' wives during the few months in summer when they gave milk, and allowed to forage for themselves during the rest of the year.

In 1839, Wisconsin farmers planted about 15,000 acres of wheat and harvested 212,116 bushels. In 1849, 306,000 acres of wheat were planted and 4,286,131 bushels harvested. Within a decade, Wisconsin had become a major wheat-growing state. By 1860, Wisconsin was second only to Illinois in wheat production, producing an amazing 29 million bushels. (Today's wheat-growing states were just being settled at this time.) Wheat farming had spread throughout the settled parts of Wisconsin—into the northeast and the sand country of central Wisconsin.[2]

From the time of statehood (1848) until well into the 1870s, Wisconsin was a wheat-growing state, with few dairy cows. Dairy farming did not begin until wheat farmers could no longer grow the crop.

Early Cheese Factories

Some dairying took place in the midst of wheat growing. It was meager by today's standards, but a harbinger of what was to come. As was true in New York and other states that raised dairy cattle, Wisconsin women cared for the cows and made cheese in their kitchens.

The earliest evidence of a commercial cheese operation was one operated by Charles Rockwell beginning in 1837, at Koshkonong, a few miles south of Fort Atkinson. Whether one could dare call it the first cheese factory in the state is debatable.

---

2. Ibid., 521, and Robert C. Nesbit, *Wisconsin: A History* (Madison, WI: University of Wisconsin Press, 1973), 273.

A few years later, another cheese operation opened near Lake Mills in Jefferson County. J. G. Pickett, who later became a cheese maker in Winnebago County, reported:

> In the year 1840, my father, Mr. A. Pickett, removed from the state of Ohio and settled near Rock Lake, in the town of Lake Mills, in this county. But a few pioneers had preceded him, and civilization in this part of the then territory of Wisconsin was in its infancy.... My father saw the opportunity, and so, in the spring of 1841, set about supplying the demand [for dairy]. He had driven from Ohio ten cows, he was satisfied that with that number he could supply the demand of the territory, and I am very confident that he had no competition in the business, but there were no cows to be bought at any price, and had there been any for sale there was no money to pay for them. But the idea suggested itself to my mother, why not cooperate with our neighbors in cheese making? It was a capital and original idea, and was at once adopted by the head of the family. We had four neighbors by this time...[and] the four families owned ten cows.[3]

Flanagan Cheese Factory (Fred Stampfle, cheese maker), northwest of Monroe on County C, Green County.

—From Historic Cheesemaking Center.

---

3. J. G. Picket, "Pioneer Dairying in Wisconsin," in D. W. Curtis, Sec., *Sixth Annual Report of the Wisconsin Dairymen's Association* (Madison, WI: Wisconsin Dairymen's Association, 1878), 96-97.

The neighbors rented their cows to the Picketts for two years. During the winter months when the cows were not milking, the neighbors kept the cows on the home farms.

J. G. Pickett and his mother began milking cows and making cheese on June 1, 1841. Pickett claimed this to be the first cooperative cheese-making arrangement in Wisconsin, begun twelve years before Jesse Williams opened his New York cheese factory in 1853. Each owner's milk was carefully weighed and credited to him each day. In the fall the cheese was divided and apportioned to the owners. It was, however, a kitchen factory operating in a log house.

These were relatively feeble cheese-making attempts and unknown to the thousands of wheat farmers making a living from the golden grain. Nonetheless, Wisconsin people were beginning to make cheese. At the first Wisconsin State Fair, held in Janesville in October 1851, seven cheese makers contributed to the cheese exhibit.

Another pioneer cheese-making operation began in Sheboygan County. John J. Smith had moved to Sheboygan Falls from New

An early cheese press used to press whey from curds and then knit them together.

—Bodenstab Cheese Factory, Sheboygan County Historical Museum, Sheboygan, 1996.

York in the summer of 1844. Earlier, the family had lived in Bucks County, Pennsylvania, and Lewis County, New York, where they farmed and operated a foundry for making plows. John J.'s father had come to Sheboygan County in the spring of 1845, and brothers J. A. and Hiram arrived on July 4, 1847. They, like almost all settlers in Wisconsin, immediately began growing wheat, planting a winter crop in 1847. The record does not show when they first got into the dairy business, but by 1858 both John J. and Hiram were milking cows. John constructed a cheese house with plastered interior walls to help control temperature and humidity. In 1858 he bought a cheese vat and began gathering unsalted curd from neighboring farms to combine with his own. He salted, pressed, and cured the cheese, but marketing it became a problem. Gustave William Buchen, in his history of Sheboygan County, reported this incident:

A barrel of cheese weighs 500 pounds. Some cheddar cheese is sold this way.

> In the autumn of 1858, Mr. Smith barreled fifty-eight cheeses, boxes not obtainable, and took them to Chicago for sale. Leaving his cheese at the warehouse, he called on the dealers and endeavored to effect a sale. On asking if they would like to purchase, he met with the inquiry, "Where was your cheese made?"
>
> "In Sheboygan."
>
> "Where is that?"
>
> "In Wisconsin."
>
> "We don't want any Wisconsin cheese; can't sell anything but New York cheese, and don't want anything else in our store."
>
> Finally, in desperation, Smith asked another cheese dealer to look at his cheese. He paid the dealer one dollar for the half hour spent examining the fifty-eight barrels. The dealer offered eight cents a pound, emphasizing that he wanted Eastern (New York) not Western cheese.[4]

Some of the difficulty John Smith faced selling his cheese was due to its low quality and lack of uniformity. It was extremely difficult to turn out a quality cheese product when curds were

---

4. Gustave William Buchen, *Historic Sheboygan County* (Sheboygan, WI: Sheboygan County Historical Society, 1944), 275-276.

collected from neighbors. Soon after, John Smith abandoned his cheese-making efforts.

A year later, in 1859, Hiram Smith and Ira N. Strong began making cheese on their farms near Sheboygan Falls. In 1861, they began collecting milk rather than curd from their neighbors, thus controlling the entire cheese-making process.

A few years later (the exact date is unknown), Hiram Smith's brother-in-law, Hiram Conover, began making cheese using a woodshed in his yard. Conover's son, Seth, helped his father. Seth traveled to Utica, New York, to learn scientific cheese making, and upon his return, Hiram Conover built a cheese factory in Plymouth that became one of the largest in the country.

Chester Hazen, cheese maker and leader in developing the dairy industry in Wisconsin.

—*From* Portrait and Biographical Album of Fond du Lac County, Wisconsin (*Acme Publishing Company, 1889*).

Chester Hazen of Fond du Lac County is often credited with establishing the first true cheese factory in Wisconsin, in 1864. Hazen, like the Smiths, came to Wisconsin from New York and settled near Ladoga, twelve miles from Fond du Lac. Hazen constructed a building that was different from those used by the Picketts and the Smiths—it was not on his farmstead. His factory was soon making cheese from more than a hundred cows. An unidentified newspaper of the day reported:

County farms branded the [Hazen] factory a "great curiosity" and flocked to watch cheese making. At times farm wagons lined up for a quarter of a mile on the road leading to "Chet" Hazen's plant. In 1865, he had, according to early historians, the "Lacteal product of 200 cows" for his cheese factory. By 1870 1,000 cows furnished the milk supply, and an 1870 report showed that the Ladoga factory produced 194,544 pounds of curd cheese.[5]

Hazen is believed to be the first cheese maker to ship Wisconsin cheese in train carloads out of the state. In 1870, he shipped the first carload of Wisconsin cheese ever sent to the New York market. Hazen worked hard, not only to supply volume but also to manufacture quality cheese. In 1878, he took first prize for factory cheese at the International Dairy Fair held in New York.

---

5. From undated records filed with the Fond du Lac Historical Society.

In recognition of his pioneer cheese-making efforts, a plaque was erected at the site of Hazen's cheese factory in Ladoga, at Highway 26 and County TC. It reads, "Erected in Honor of Chester Hazen, Father of Wisconsin's Cheese Industry. Erected a Factory on this site, 1864."

The question of who built the first cheese factory in Wisconsin will likely never be settled. Some claim that Charles Rockwell from Jefferson County was first; others say that the Picketts' community cheese-making efforts should be honored. Others believe John and Hiram Smith of Sheboygan County should receive the nod. And many more argue that Chester Hazen's cheese factory in Fond du Lac County, because it was a freestanding building off the farmstead and because it clearly was a large commercial operation, ought to be recognized as first. But agreeing on which cheese factory was first isn't nearly as important as recognizing that a great agricultural transition occurred in Wisconsin, and that the emerging cheese factories were symbols of it.

Chester Hazen's cheese factory in Fond du Lac County, which began operating in 1864. Some people have claimed that this was the first commercial cheese factory in the state.

—From Illustrated Atlas Map, Fond du Lac County, Wisconsin *(Harney and Tucker, 1874).*

Wheat to Cheese

After the railroad came to Wisconsin in the 1850s, wheat growing spread rapidly. Transporting wheat from farm to mill had long been a problem, but now the railroads could easily haul grain to the great flour mills in La Crosse, Milwaukee, and the Fox River Valley. Between 1858 and 1870, grain and flour sales at Milwaukee mills quadrupled. Wheat and flour made up three-fourths of the railroad's traffic between 1850 and 1870.[6]

6. Lampard, *The Rise of the Dairy Industry in Wisconsin*, 40.

From the earliest days of settlement to well past the Civil War, wheat farming was the predominant agricultural activity in Wisconsin. However, as the years passed, ominous signs appeared on the horizon. As wheat was planted year after year on the same land, yields decreased, even in fertile southern Wisconsin. Weather was a problem too: when there was not enough rain, the crop wouldn't develop well; too much rain or rainfall at the wrong time and the wheat rotted in the field. The chinch bug (a little insect with an X on its back and a long beak that sucks the juices from wheat plants) infested some fields, leaving little wheat to harvest. Moreover, the markets were never predictable.

Economics eventually drove farmers to shift from growing wheat to milking dairy cows. But why dairy cows and not sheep or beef cattle or even some other crop? Actually, a number of south-central Wisconsin farmers saw hops (an ingredient in beer making) as the answer. Sauk County became the center of the hops-growing industry, with 1867 a peak year. Then the market collapsed and prices never returned. Other farmers experimented with tobacco, but tobacco growing in southern and southwestern Wisconsin was never more than an adjunct to other agricultural pursuits. Potato growing, another possibility, was suited to only a few counties in central Wisconsin. Sheep raising had become somewhat popular beginning in the 1840s and boomed during the Civil War years, when the demand for wool was great. After the Civil War, wool prices dropped and farmers left sheep raising behind.

Initially, a scant few farmers took up dairying. Dairy farming was a challenge. The prevalent breed of cattle, Durhams (today we call them milking shorthorns), were bred as dual- or even triple-purpose animals. They provided milk and meat, and even pulled plows and other farm implements. As is often true, that which is supposedly multipurpose often fails in all purposes. This was true of the Durham cow. She gave milk for two or three summer months, dried up, and remained dry throughout the winter. Some farmers preferred this arrangement. Who wanted to milk a cow the year-round, especially during the winter?

Farmers quickly realized that for a cow to milk more than enough to satisfy its calf, it needed good feed. Rustling around in the woods searching for whatever it could find did not contribute

A young cheese maker and his wife next to a hanging cheese kettle. He was obviously proud of both.

—From Historic Cheesemaking Center.

to greater milk production.

And a cultural problem—a problem even larger than questionable economics and difficult management—loomed. For generations, caring for cows and making cheese and butter had been women's work. If the man on the farm wanted dairying to become a major source of income, then he would have to participate. For the longtime wheat farmer, working with cows and milk was beneath his dignity. He was a man of the soil. He planted the crops, harvested them, and sold them. He earned money for the family. In his opinion, caring for cows was domestic work. It earned little or no money and mainly provided some food for the table. Besides, he thought, tradition should prevail. There was men's work and there was women's work and these should not be confused. This was the dilemma many wheat farmers faced after the Civil War, when prices dropped, yields declined, and even worse, insect and disease problems emerged. Wheat farming was clearly on the way out, but the switch to dairying did not happen quickly; it took nearly twenty-five years. Slowly, farmers got over the notion that caring for cows was women's work. Economics forced them to change: Either move to dairying or give up farming.

Wisconsin Dairymen's Association

By the early 1870s, Chester Hazen, Hiram Smith and a number of other dairy farmers became convinced that dairying was the future for Wisconsin. To make the point, these and other dairy farmers organized the Wisconsin Dairymen's Association, after strong encouragement from William Dempster Hoard, who called for such an organization in his newspaper, the *Jefferson County Union.*

Number of cheese factories in Wisconsin:

1870-90
1880-700
1890-1,149
1905-1,518
1922-2,807
1938-1,917
1950-1,279
1960-798
1980-334
1995-142

Dairy farmers from throughout Wisconsin gathered at the Lindon House in Watertown on Thursday, February 15, 1872. Many of them had switched from wheat growing to milking cows, but now some of them wondered about the wisdom of their decision. Most of the milk from their cows was made into cheese, and cheese prices were not good.

It seemed clear that they had a common problem—inadequate returns for their efforts—and perhaps an organization might help them solve it. As the group took their seats at the Lindon House, there was grumbling and complaining about milking cows. "Should have stuck with raising wheat," more than one farmer was heard to say.

Chester Hazen of Ladoga was quickly elected president pro tem for the meeting. Following Hazen's election, W. D. Hoard agreed to serve as secretary. Mr. S. Faville of Lake Mills, president of the Northwestern Dairymen's Association, stood up and began stating the reasons for the meeting.

"The dairyman of this state," he began, "has long felt the necessity for some united action with regard to the marketing of dairy products. As the matter now stands, the producers of butter and cheese are at the mercy of a disorganized market."

"That's right," someone said from over by the window, nodding his head in agreement. Other heads were nodding, as well.

"What we need," Faville continued, "is cooperative action on the part of dairymen. They've done this in New York State, and we can do it here."

G. E. Morrow, editor of the *Western Farmer,* asked to speak. "I have a great interest in what you are planning to do," he said. "If the activities of this organization are taken hold of with intelligence and earnestness of purpose, a much improved state of affairs will result."

More nods of agreement from the group.

After some discussion, the group voted to organize a state dairymen's association, and proceeded to elect Chester Hazen as president.

President Hazen then addressed the group.

"We've got to think well beyond Wisconsin when we talk about marketing our cheese, and we've got to listen to what out-of-state markets want. St. Louis wants a soft cheese, weighing about sixty pounds. New York wants a harder cheese that is slightly colored. Chicago prefers cheese that is made in a thirteen-inch hoop. And in the Liverpool, England, market, cheese that is made in a four-teen-inch hoop and weighing about fifty pounds will bring a half cent more per pound."

Everyone listened intently to this interesting and new informa-tion. The cheese-making industry was becoming complicated. To sell their cheese, farmers and cheese makers were going to have to pay attention to the demands of the marketplace.

The group discussed marketing approaches followed in New York State. They passed the following resolution before day's end: "That the Executive Committee be directed to appoint two days each month, in which a butter and cheese market shall be held in some convenient building, in Watertown, and to make all neces-sary arrangements therefore." A constitution was presented and promptly signed by more than twenty members in attendance before they adjourned.[7]

In addition to worrying about marketing cheese and calming fears of former wheat farmers, the Wisconsin Dairymen's Association worked to encourage others to become dairy farmers, and for all dairy farmers and cheese makers to produce a quality product. The unmarketable quality of some cheese had become a major problem for the fledgling industry.

At their third meeting, held in Fort Atkinson on February 17 and 18, 1875, President Hazen was late, as were several other mem-bers, because of a huge snowstorm that prevented the trains from running. Upon arrival, Hazen made the following comments:

"I hope to see the time when the quality of our Wisconsin but-ter and cheese will all come up to the standard of excellence of the very best who are producing at the present time, and when our

---

7. "Convention of the Dairymen of Wisconsin," *Jefferson County Union*, February 23, 1872.

dairy products will be second in quality to no state in the Union."

He went on to compare dairy farming with wheat farming. "On the whole I think the dairy production much better this past season than wheat raising. The dairy production of Wisconsin, the past season, will amount to 13,000,000 pounds of cheese from 300 factories. In 1863, it was about 10,000,000 pounds of cheese. I believe the dairy products of the U.S. exceed that of any other branch of agriculture.

"The aim of a good dairyman should be to excel or take the first rank in his profession," Hazen added. To move to the "first rank" Hazen said dairy farmers should select the best dairy cows they could find, provide them with good shelter, feed them regularly in summer and winter, make sure they have plenty of pure water, and milk them at regular times. He concluded by saying, "Dairymen stand in the front rank of the agriculturists in America. Let us elevate our standard in the position it rightfully belongs, and maintain it by adding influence and dignity to our calling."[8]

Marketing cheese and other dairy products had long been a national problem, especially for New York cheese makers. In 1866, a group of Eastern cheese makers organized the American Dairy Association (ADA) to seek out export markets for butter and, especially, cheese. The organization also looked for new U.S. markets, but knew it was facing difficult odds. Americans enjoyed butter and ate lots of it, but cheese was seen as a relish to be eaten only on special occasions.

In 1876, the American Dairy Association asked the Wisconsin Dairymen's Association to participate in an exhibit at the Centennial Exhibition in Philadelphia. The Wisconsin people were cool toward the idea. "Hoard argued vehemently against trusting 'the honor and reputation of Wisconsin' in the hands of this self-styled 'American Association' which, he alleged, was a mere knot of New York Dairymen."[9]

Thus, Wisconsin dairymen began putting aside their feelings of inadequacy and stretched their wings. They stood up to the New Yorkers, who for many years had been the nation's leaders in dairying and cheese making.

---

8. *Third Annual Report of the Wisconsin Dairymen's Association* (Fort Atkinson, WI: W. B. Hoard, printer, 1875), 11-14.

9. Lampard, *The Rise of the Dairy Industry in Wisconsin*, 138.

Why the Cheese Factory?

Because cheese making had for centuries been a home activity, many people, especially men, thought it should stay that way. As the state's first cheese factories emerged, strong arguments were made both for and against the factory approach to cheese making.

Having cheese factories meant milk had to be hauled to a central location where a cheese maker made the milk into cheese. Farmers did not like the idea of hauling their milk to a central location, sometimes two or three or more miles away, in all kinds of weather. Country roads were so dusty the wagon drivers could scarcely breathe. Sometimes the vehicles were buried in snow or stuck in a quagmire of mud. From the time the railroads came into the state in the 1850s and 1860s until well after 1900, little was done to improve rural roads.

Farmers also had to be on time at the factory or risk having their milk rejected. The cheese maker needed all of the milk in the vat when he started making cheese. A farmer could not drag in late with a litany of excuses. Former wheat farmers had been accustomed to making their own hours; many did not like having someone else set the schedule.

Most factories insisted on a high level of cleanliness; some farmers didn't like spending so much time washing pails and cans. And many of the early factories only operated seven or eight months of the year because most cows only milked during the

Tools used in an early cheddar cheese factory. The cheese vat was made of wood with a metal liner.

—Bodenstab Cheese Factory, Sheboygan County Historical Museum, 1996.

warmer months. If a farmer produced milk when the cheese factory was closed, he had to make his own cheese or use the milk for other purposes.

But for most, cheese factories offered far more advantages than kitchen operations. The cheese produced in a factory was uniform and generally of higher quality; thus, it usually commanded a higher price. One person, a cheese maker, could devote all his time to cheese making. Others took over the job of marketing, usually a mystery to those making cheese in their kitchens.

Women, as might be guessed, were most happy with cheese factories. Cheese making could be removed from their kitchens. Mrs. E. P. Allerton spoke at the third annual meeting of the Wisconsin Dairymen's Association. She wanted to make sure the audience of mostly men understood the woman's viewpoint.

> The simplest and most primitive [method of making cheese] was after this fashion: The milk and whey were heated in the kitchen boiler; the curd was set in a tub, and drained through a concern that was called a "cheese ladder." The press was a lever wedged under a beam of the woodshed, with a big stone on the end for the power, and the cheese for a fulcrum…. The object would appear to be the prying up of the wood-shed, but no, it was to press the cheese…. In many farmhouses, the dairy work loomed up every year, a mountain that it took all summer to scale. But the mountain is removed; it has been hauled over to the cheese factory, and let us be thankful time does not hang heavy on the hands of the farmer's wife now that it is gone. She did not need the dairy work for recreation.[10]

William Dempster Hoard

During this period, former New Yorkers were clearly making a difference in Wisconsin's dairy industry. The aforementioned Hiram Smith and Chester Hazen were prominent. So was William Dempster Hoard.

Hoard was born October 10, 1836, on a farm in central New York. Hoard set out for Wisconsin in 1859 and first lived with his cousin on a farm fifteen miles north of Watertown. After serving

---

10. *Third Annual Report of the Wisconsin Dairymen's Association*, 17-18.

in the Union Army during the Civil War, he traveled back to Wisconsin to grow hops. When the hops market crashed, Hoard was financially ruined, owing some $2,000. He tried to sell washing machines in Iowa, with little success. He switched to selling musical instruments, but with a wife and three children back in Wisconsin, he decided to return home.

Young Hoard got the idea that he might enjoy newspaper work. When he returned from Iowa he began writing for the *Watertown Republican*, but he wanted his own paper. On March 7, 1870, the first issue of the *Jefferson County Union* came off the presses. It was a tiny, four-page weekly that Hoard printed on the *Watertown Republican* presses. He was constantly on the road selling subscriptions to farmers for his paper.

In 1885, William Dempster Hoard of Fort Atkinson started Hoard's Dairyman, *a publication devoted to the dairy farmer. It is still published today.*

Hoard did not forget his love for the dairy cow, which had developed when he lived in New York State. He viewed himself as both an editor and a dairy leader, and he saw his newspaper as a way to educate farmers. When the Wisconsin Dairymen's Association organized in 1872, Hoard became active in it. In 1885, Hoard, along with his son, Arthur, decided to start a newspaper devoted to the dairy farmer. On the advice of a friend, he called it "Hoard's Dairyman." It was included as a four-page supplement in the *Union*. Farmers also could subscribe separately. *Hoard's Dairyman* became the official organ of the Wisconsin Dairymen's Association.

Soon, Hoard's modest little newspaper became an important voice for dairy farming across the country, and in other parts of the world as well. Along the way, Hoard purchased his own 193-acre farm near Fort Atkinson and began to share his experiences in his newspaper. *Hoard's Dairyman* continues to be published in Fort Atkinson.[11]

Cheese Factory Numbers Increase

Between 1869 and 1879, wheat farming declined dramatically, from an annual crop of 525,000 bushels to 193,000 bushels.[12] Henry Bakken, a University of Wisconsin agricultural economist, estimated that in 1860 approximately thirty cheese factories in the

---

11. Loren H. Osman, *W. D. Hoard: A Man For His Time* (Fort Atkinson, WI: W. D. Hoard and Sons Company, 1985).

12. Lampard, *The Rise of the Dairy Industry in Wisconsin*, 112.

Grand View Cheese Factory (Conrad Frehner family, cheese makers), southeast of Belmont, Lafayette County, c. 1913.

—From Jacob Frehner.

state were making American cheese (mostly cheddar). By 1870, the number had climbed to ninety; by 1880 it was 700.[13]

Cheese factories rapidly increased in eastern and southern Wisconsin. By 1870, twenty-five cheese factories operated in Sheboygan County. Seven years later, the county had sixty-two cheese factories. In 1878, Sheboygan County's factories produced 5.8 million pounds of cheese. About forty percent was exported to Liverpool, England. The average price received was 7.5 cents per pound.[14]

Green County Cheese Making

During the late 1800s, most eastern Wisconsin cheese factories were making cheddar cheese, but factories producing foreign types of cheese were also taking their place in the state. Foreign cheese was primarily Swiss and Limburger. Some Green County cheese factories made Swiss cheese, but more factories made Limburger, which especially appealed to the Germans and Swiss. In 1880, writer John Luchisinger wrote that twenty-five cheese

---

13. Henry H. Bakken, *American Cheese Factories in Wisconsin*, Research Bulletin 100, University of Wisconsin Agricultural Experiment Station (August 1930), 2.

14. Edwin Fisher, *The Cheese Factories of Sheboygan County* (Sheboygan, WI: Sheboygan County Historical Society, 1992), 11.

factories in Green County made Limburger cheese, "a premeditated outrage upon the organs of smell."[15]

The Swiss had raised cows almost as soon as they settled in Green County. The first cattle were driven from Ohio in 1846, enough so that each family could have one cow. An 1846 livestock inventory of Green County reported one bull, eighteen cows, fifteen heifers, and twenty-five calves.[16]

Swiss immigrants had also brought with them their knowledge of cheese making and their taste for good cheese. But they, like other immigrants who settled in Wisconsin, got caught up in the wheat-growing craze. The Swiss who settled in Green County planted acre upon acre of wheat—and they did little else but grow wheat until 1870. When wheat growing collapsed, the Swiss, along with other southern Wisconsin wheat growers, looked to dairy farming as an alternative. Conrad Zimmerman, who wrote an 1884 history of New Glarus, said, "Either cheese or nothing, and happily we got cheese. The old wheat fields were seeded with clover and grass. Cows were put on them. Cheese factories were built. After the fact was proved that there was a ready market for cheese, it only took five or six years until cheese making was the main branch of work for the whole farming population. It not only pays better but the farms are constantly more productive."[17]

One of several types of wooden cheese boxes used to store and ship cheese.

Rudolph Benkert came to Monroe in 1867 and is recorded as Green County's first cheese maker. He started making Limburger cheese, which he cured in the cellar of his home. John Marty was another early Green County cheese maker. He began making a round Swiss-style cheese in 1868, selling it in Madison. But the person credited with establishing the first cheese factory in Green County is Nicholas Gerber. Gerber, a native of Switzerland, came to America in 1857, first settling in New York State where he made Limburger. He came to Green County in 1868, and built and equipped a Limburger cheese factory in the town of New Glarus. The next year, Gerber started the first Swiss cheese factory in Washington Township.

15. Lampard, *The Rise of the Dairy Industry in Wisconsin*, 113.

16. Emory A. Odell, *Swiss Cheese Industry* (Monroe, WI: Monroe Evening Times, 1936), 7.

17. Ibid., 6.

Gerber had learned factory cheese operations in New York and Ohio and soon expanded his operations. At one time, he had eight cheese factories in New Glarus and Washington Townships, and he purchased cheese from other small factories in the area. By 1876, Washington Township had fourteen cheese factories. Emory Odell, a Monroe newspaper editor, said this about Nicholas Gerber:

> Children of the first dairymen still living hereabouts have pleasant memories of this kindly man as he traveled the country by horse and buggy to his cheese factories, as this was the only way he had of keeping in touch with them. The struggling dairymen welcomed his visits as they were mutually interested in an improvement of conditions and relations existing between them were the best. Mr. Gerber wore a long black beard and always drove a white horse hitched to a single buggy. He made regular trips over the road in New Glarus and Washington Townships where he carried on his principal operations.[18]

Nicholas Gerber died in 1903, but he was long remembered by Green County cheese makers and farmers for his many contributions.

Making the Transition

The shift from wheat growing to caring for dairy cattle was more than some wheat farmers could accept. But there were few alternatives. Some wheat farmers moved west, to Kansas and Nebraska, and to North and South Dakota to continue growing wheat. Most stayed in Wisconsin—and they listened to the New Yorkers, such as Chester Hazen, Hiram Smith, and William Hoard, who continued promoting dairy farming. Many of these same farmers continued hoping that one day they could return to growing wheat. It would not happen.

---

18. Ibid., 12-13.

4 *Rapid Expansion: 1880-1920*

In the 1880s, dairy cows began grazing in former wheat fields, and dairy barns began appearing alongside horse barns. As the number of dairy cows increased, so did cheese production.

By 1885, 1,000 cheese factories were operating in the state. Five years later, there were 1,149. The leading cheese-making counties were Fond du Lac (with 117 factories), Sheboygan (107), Green (104), Manitowoc (76), and Dodge (60).[1] Wisconsin cheese production reached 60 million pounds in 1900, and by 1915, the state was making nearly 235 million pounds annually.[2]

In 1899, Wisconsin produced 26.6 percent of the nation's cheese. By 1909, it was 46.6 percent, and in 1919, 63.1 percent. In 1910, Wisconsin pushed aside New York to become the nation's leading cheese-producing state. Wisconsin continues in that role today.

The University of Wisconsin and Dairying

The University of Wisconsin opened in 1849; as early as 1851, the university's first chancellor, John H. Lathrop, spoke of the need for agricultural education. The legislature listened but provided no funding. In 1862, Congress passed the Morrill Act, which

---

1. *Annual Report of the Dairy and Food Commissioner* (Madison, WI: Office of the Dairy and Food Commissioner, 1892), 55-63.

2. H. L. Russell, "Dairy Industry in Wisconsin," Research Bulletin 88, University of Wisconsin Agricultural Experiment Station (September 1901), 5, and Lampard, *The Rise of the Dairy Industry in Wisconsin*, 227, 255.

provided federal land grants for establishing agricultural and mechanical arts colleges, but the University of Wisconsin waited until after the Civil War to take advantage of it. Finally, in 1866, the legislature created a professorship of agriculture and chemistry in the College of Arts. The university regents also accepted 195 acres on the west side of the campus (a donation from Dane County) for an experimental farm.

The new agricultural instructional program was essentially a failure. "Too bookish," farmers said. "We want something practical, information that can help us with our problems." Many farmers also believed that sending their sons to the university meant sending them away from the land.

By 1870, farm leaders were calling for a College of Agriculture that was separate from the university and located in a city other than Madison. In 1878, the Wisconsin Dairymen's Association petitioned Governor William E. Smith to appoint farmers to the University of Wisconsin Board of Regents; Hiram Smith was soon appointed to that position. He immediately argued that the University of Wisconsin should do more for Wisconsin

Students learning the cheese-making process at the University of Wisconsin College of Agriculture Dairy Short Course, c. 1900. Cheese-making facilities were located in Hiram Smith Hall. The Dairy Short Course was instituted in 1889.

—From University of Wisconsin-Madison Archives.

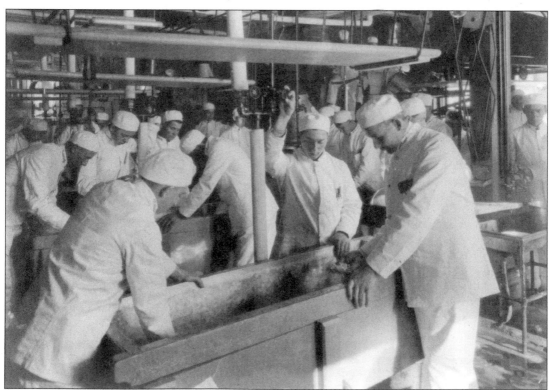

agriculture. By 1880, Hiram Smith had convinced university officials to appoint W. A. Henry as professor of agriculture on the Madison campus. Henry organized the Farm Short Course in 1886 and began a series of farmers' institutes wherein university professors traveled around the state, meeting directly with farm groups. Henry also pushed for the establishment of an agricultural experiment station on the Madison campus. The experiment station began operations on March 27, 1883, after the legislature passed a tax bill to fund it. The need for well-researched information had become evident—information that ranged from how to build a dairy barn and what to feed a cow, to how to store cheese and new approaches for selling it.

With continued pressure from agricultural leaders, especially the Wisconsin Dairymen's Association, the legislature officially established the College of Agriculture in 1889. The new college was challenged to reach out to farmers and others interested in agriculture. However, few students enrolled in the new four-year academic program. During the 1899-1900 school year, nine students enrolled. In contrast, the more practical Farm Short Course had enrolled 102 students in 1895.[3]

In 1889, the College of Agriculture also launched a short course designed for cheese and butter makers interested in improving their skills. The Dairy School, a 12-week program, enrolled two students in 1890. They met in a little frame building at the university farm in Madison. The following year, 70 students enrolled. In his biennial report, W. A. Henry, now dean of the College of Agriculture, explained that the rapid increase in numbers was due to "the discovery or invention of the Babcock Milk Test [a simple but accurate method for measuring the butterfat content of milk], which greatly increased the interest of dairymen, and especially buttermakers, in their vocation.... There was no way, before the Babcock test came out, to accurately and quickly measure how much fat there was in patrons' milk...."[4]

In 1891, the twelve-week Dairy Short Course curriculum included four courses:

---

3. W. H. Glover, *Farm and College: The College of Agriculture of the University of Wisconsin, A History* (Madison, WI: University of Wisconsin Press, 1952), 232, 239.

4. W. A. Henry, "The Wisconsin Dairy School And Its Work," *Biennial Report of the Dairy and Food Commissioner of Wisconsin for 1899-1900* (Madison, WI: Office of the Dairy and Food Commissioner, 1901), 74.

1. Milk constitution, churning, milk testing, milk preservatives (twenty lectures).

2. Milk testing, detection of watering, skimming, payment for milk (prerequisite for courses 3 and 4).

3. Butter making: farm cream separation (hand and power), butter extractor, testing skim milk and buttermilk, grading, comparison of butter made by students with commercial products (four weeks).

4. Cheese making: methods, management of curing rooms, testing, grading (eight weeks).

Dean Henry's description of the short course included this information:

Beginning in 1916, Wisconsin cheese makers were required to have a license to make cheese.

> Each student must before entering the school have worked at least four months in a creamery or cheese factory. During [the time in the dairy school], he will learn much concerning factory operations and familiarize himself with dairy methods in general, with tools, apparatus, etc.... The order of the day is as follows: At eight o'clock in the morning the students assemble for a lecture, which lasts from eight o'clock to eight-fifty. By nine o'clock the class has separated in its four divisions: the first section, numbering one-fourth of the students, repairs to the cheese room for instruction in the making of cheese; section II goes to the creamery for instruction in butter making; section III repairs to the laboratory on the third floor for work in milk testing, while section IV passes to an adjoining building where instruction is given in the care and management of the boiler, the steam engine, also in pipe cutting, pipe fitting, soldering, and belt lacing. About thirty students work in each section. The work continues until twelve o'clock. The cheese making naturally goes longer. In the afternoon students return for instruction in the making of starters for the creamery and cheese factory, for additional work with engines, etc.[5]

5. Ibid., 75-76.

Students in these early dairy schools were mature men with an average age of thirty. The Dairy Short Course became extremely successful. By 1901, 1,142 students had attended or were attending, and 240 had been awarded graduation certificates. According to Dean Henry, women were admitted "on the same terms as men, and each class has some women in it learning the trade."[6]

The university built Hiram Smith Hall, a new dairy building, in 1891 at a cost of $45,000. Machinery and instructional apparatus cost an additional $12,000. It became a busy processing plant, producing cheddar, Swiss, brick, Limburger, Edam, and Gouda cheese, fancy print butter, pasteurized cream, and pasteurized milk. In 1900, the dairy school plant processed 3 million pounds of milk. The plant sold butter in Madison, Chicago, and other cities. It sold pasteurized cream in Madison, Milwaukee, and Chicago. The value of the products sold in 1900 was $39,000.[7]

As part of their responsibilities, dairy school students were required to wash down the dairy laboratory each day. The men resented this. Some of them managed cheese plants at home that

Dairy Short Course students at the University of Wisconsin College of Agriculture learning how to test milk using the Babcock Milk Test, c. 1900.

—*From University of Wisconsin-Madison Archives.*

6. Ibid., 77.

7. Ibid., 76.

Sketch of the first Babcock Milk Tester. Stephen Moulton Babcock, professor at the University of Wisconsin, invented the milk tester in 1890. It measured the fat content of milk and provided a standardized way of paying farmers for their milk.

handled more than 20,000 pounds of milk daily. Why should they have to do this menial work as part of their training? One of the dairy school instructors replied that the greatest problem many cheese makers had was keeping their plants clean. So the students were trained to clean and the training left its mark. Cheese buyers later noted that they could recognize a factory run by a Dairy Short Course graduate by its cleanliness.[8]

The Agricultural Experiment Station, which opened in 1883, also was beginning to make important contributions to Wisconsin's fledgling dairy industry, on the farm and in cheese manufacturing plants. One of the most influential researchers was Stephen Moulton Babcock.

Babcock came to the university in 1888, and began work in the station. He had studied at Cornell University in New York, and had earned a PhD from the University of Gottingen in Germany. Babcock immediately began investigating animal nutrition that would lead to greater milk production. He, together with Harry Russell, another professor of agriculture, developed a process for the cold curing of cheese, a process that reduced spoilage and resulted in more consistent quality in the final product.

Babcock's most important work, however, was developing the Babcock Milk Test in 1890. This test accurately measured the fat content of milk using sulfuric acid and a special centrifuge. Before this time, dairy plants had no easy way of measuring the fat content of milk, and no uniform way of paying farmers for their milk. Some farmers, accidentally or on purpose, added water to their milk; others skimmed off the cream for home use. With the Babcock test, there was now an accurate and easy way to tell if farmers had tampered with their milk.

Babcock, a very unassuming researcher, never patented his invention. He believed that dairy manufacturers should have easy access to it. Within a short time the Babcock test was widely adapted and used in milk plants across the country. In an Agricultural Experiment Station report, Babcock wrote, "Whether this test will find a place among those [tests] already introduced, time alone can decide. In the hope that it

---

8. W. H. Glover, *Farm and College*, 228-233.

Stephen Moulton Babcock invented the Babcock Milk Tester in 1890. This is a more modern version of the tester that was used for many years in the dairy industry.

may benefit some who are striving to improve their stock and enable creameries to avoid the evils of the present system, the test is given to the public."[9]

H. L. Russell was another researcher at the Agricultural Experiment Station. He was the first scholar in the country to earn a PhD in bacteriology. His research called attention to the perils of tuberculosis in cattle, and led to tuberculin testing, beginning in 1894. Russell also helped promote pasteurization of milk, and by 1896, university researchers had developed techniques for using lactic acid bacteria (starter cultures) to make cheese from pasteurized rather than raw milk. This new method contributed greatly to the manufacture of higher quality cheese. It also meant cheese could be safely consumed as soon as it was made. Today, cheese made from raw milk must be aged for a minimum of sixty days, during which time the natural curing process of the cheese eliminates harmful organisms that may be present in nonpasteurized milk.

9. Stephen M. Babcock, "A New Method for the Estimation of Fat in Milk, Especially Adapted to Creameries and Cheese Factories," *Seventh Annual Report of the Agricultural Experiment Station* (Madison, WI, 1890), 98-113.

Over the years, the College of Agriculture at the University of Wisconsin-Madison continued to make many contributions to the dairy industry and improvements in cheese making, and it does so today.

Dairying in Northern Wisconsin

The development of dairying in northern Wisconsin (that is, north of a line extending roughly from Green Bay to Eau Claire), was different from that in the southern and eastern counties of the state. This was the land of the big pines, thousands of acres of them. During the peak wheat-growing years in southern Wisconsin, lumbermen were sawing down trees in the north. Land once graced with pine trees became a stark landscape of giant stumps.

Some owners of this stump-strewn land considered growing wheat. But by that time, disease, low yields, and pests had already wreaked havoc with thousands of acres of wheat in southern Wisconsin. And wheat farmers were already looking to the dairy cow as an alternative to wheat growing.

Agricultural leaders, convinced that wheat growing should not be attempted in the north, advocated dairy farming on these once tree- studded lands.

On northern Wisconsin's richer soils, the plowman followed the woodcutter. Soon dairy barns appeared and milk cows grazed in pastures that had once supported giant white pines. Professor H. L. Russell of the University of Wisconsin believed the northern counties had some definite advantages for dairy farmers and cheese makers. In 1901 he wrote,

> One great advantage, which this region possesses...is that a clover crop is rarely subject to failure. In the southern counties the snow falls often so light that clover winter-kills, and it is therefore difficult at times to secure luxuriant pasturage and maintain the fertility of the soil. In the central and northern counties this has not yet happened, and the result is that these highly nitrogenous forage crops can be raised in great abundance.
>
> Many portions of this region are also abundantly supplied with springs and flowing streams, the temperature of which is often as low as 50 degrees F., and in some regions

even lower. With these conditions it is possible to keep milk in much better condition than in a hot dry climate.

Russell also saw some definite advantages for cheese makers who operated factories in the northern regions of the state. "It is now a well ascertained fact that the best quality of cheese is made where the curing changes go on slowly at considerably lower temperatures than has hitherto been customary…. The natural temperature environment [for curing cheese] approximates somewhat closely that needed for the process. The ability to use natural ice in comparison with artificial refrigeration…renders the control of this problem in this and similar regions comparatively easy.[10]

Problems in the Cheese Vat

In the late 1800s, cheese production was on the increase, markets were adequate, and prices were reasonable. Dairy farmers and cheese makers were making money. But then, as too often happens, a few greedy people began taking short cuts. Would anyone notice if a few gallons of water were mixed in with the milk? Would anyone care if skim milk was used for cheese making, and then lard or stale butter added back to make up the lack of butterfat? This adulterated cheese became known as "filled cheese" and soon made its way into the export market.

Pasteurization of milk began on a commercial basis in 1913.

Filled cheese was difficult to distinguish from whole-milk cheese when it was fresh, but it aged poorly and lost much of its flavor with time. When the exported cheese arrived in England, much of it was unfit for consumption. The London market complained loudly, and export sales dropped. The Wisconsin Dairymen's Association, well aware of the problem, petitioned the legislature to establish an office to search out those who were adulterating butter and cheese. The office of the Dairy and Food Commissioner opened in 1889. In his first report, Commissioner H. C. Thom wrote:

There is not an article of commerce that requires greater skill in handling in order to secure favorable markets. No industry has been so perverted. No business exists that has been so basely manipulated, and no article of food has been

---

10. Russell, "Dairy Industry in Wisconsin," 5-6.

It takes about ten pounds of milk to produce one pound of cheese.

so degraded by counterfeiters. In no time has the honest manufacturer met with such dishonest competition. Matters have come to such a pass that the genuine article is under the ban of suspicion at home and abroad. The result has been that the subject has been thoroughly investigated by importers and steps have been taken to reduce the exportation of filled cheese from the United States.[11]

Strong words. The commissioner followed with action. Violators were warned, and several were fined $50 each. Filled cheese began disappearing, and Wisconsin's cheese reputation slowly returned after several rocky years.

Some farmers tried to make more money by adding water to their milk before hauling it to the cheese factory. The Dairy and Food Commissioner's office had some suggestions for cheese factories on how to handle this situation:

> In case any milk furnished should be of such doubtful quality as to warrant the assumption that it has been adulterated, a committee appointed by the Directors [of the cheese factory] shall visit the premises of the patron, see his cows milked morning and evening, and have the quality of such milk compared with the record of the tests made of the milk which he was previously furnishing, and if a substantial difference in quality is evident, it shall be optional with the Directors as to whether they shall (1) prosecute the patron according to law, (2) effect a settlement with him upon the payment to the funds of the manufacturer, of such a sum as may be agreed upon, or (3) exclude the patron from the privileges of the factory for a stated number of years.[12]

Wisconsin's strict quality standards and inspection procedures probably saved the state's cheese industry. By the turn of the century, cheese sales were again on the upswing. Commissioner J. Q. Emery wrote in 1906,

---

11. H. C. Thom, *First Annual Report of the State Dairy and Food Commissioner* (Madison, WI: Office of the State Dairy and Food Commissioner, 1890), 18-19.

12. Adams, *Biennial Report of the Dairy and Food Commissioner, 1895-1896*, 212.

Wisconsin is among the foremost dairy states of the union. In the extent and variety of her dairy products, she is excelled by none. The policy of our state in the inspection of cheese factories and creameries is akin to that of the national government in the recently enacted law for the inspection of meat packing establishments. Securing modern scientific practices, it tends to give the consumers cleanliness and purity in dairy products and consequent greater remuneration to those engaged in the dairy industry. It is wisdom upon the part of the state to carry into effect a policy which secures these results.[13]

Maintaining quality standards was a challenge at the turn of the century, and continues to be so to this day. However, as dairy leaders know, unless quality is maintained at a high level, there is no hope of creating and keeping markets.

Development of Process Cheese

In 1904, John L. Kraft, after several years of experimentation and study, developed Process cheese. To make Process cheese, an assortment of cheddar cheeses are ground together, pasteurized, mixed with emulsifying salt, and heated. In the early years, the mixture was placed into foil-lined containers while still hot, and then sealed.[14]

Kraft's Process cheese became one of the most popular dairy items of all time. The cheese was always the same in texture and taste, and it cut easily. It was developed at a time when there were no home refrigerators, and could be stored in an icebox, or even on the pantry shelf with no cooling necessary. Many children, who did not like the stronger taste of cheddar cheese, relished Process cheese. In addition, Process cheese was often less expensive than regular cheese.

Lovers of good cheese, though, rolled their eyes when offered Process cheese because they knew how much flavor was missing in the bland version. Some were reluctant to admit that Process cheese was even cheese.

---

13. J. Q. Emery, *Biennial Report of the Dairy and Food Commissioner* (Madison, WI: Office of the Dairy and Food Commissioner, 1906), 9.

14. Lampard, *The Rise of the Dairy Industry in Wisconsin*, 223.

Increasing Numbers

Eastern and southern Wisconsin counties produced the most milk and cheese in the early 1900s. By 1905, Sheboygan boasted 120 cheese factories manufacturing 11.6 million pounds of cheese, which was then selling for an average price of eleven cents per pound.[15]

By 1910, cheese factories operated nearly everywhere in the state. Green County had 213, Dodge County had 141, Iowa County had 128, Lafayette County had 118, and Sheboygan County had 111. Other counties with fifty or more cheese factories included Outagamie (99), Dane (92), Fond du Lac (69), Kewaunee (63), Shawano (62), Marathon (61), Calumet (54), and Clark (50).[16]

The counties with few factories were the central sand counties of Adams, Marquette, and Monroe; the far northern counties of Ashland, Bayfield, Douglas, Price, Rusk, Sawyer, and Washburn; and the southeastern counties of Milwaukee, Racine, and Kenosha. All of these counties combined had only eight cheese factories.

Four southern Wisconsin counties accounted for twenty-nine percent of the state's cheese factories. Five eastern counties accounted for another twenty-one percent. Thus, eastern and

A farmer dumping milk through the factory's intake door; note the whey barrels. Van Matre Factory (also known as Pleasant View), one and a half miles from the Wisconsin state line in Stephenson County, Illinois.

—From Historic Cheesemaking Center.

15. Edwin Fisher, *The Cheese Factories of Sheboygan County* (Sheboygan, WI: Sheboygan County Historical Society, 1992), 11.

16. J. Q. Emery, *Report of the Dairy and Food Commissioner* (Madison, WI: Office of the Dairy and Food Commissioner, 1910), 279.

southern counties accounted for half of all the cheese factories operating in the state in 1910.

Caring for the Dairy Cow

Just before and after the turn of the century, farmers built thousands of dairy barns, many of which still stand as testimony to their efforts. The barns were not inexpensive, costing upwards of $2,000 each—a lot of money in 1900. Most dairy farmers built bank barns. Cattle were housed in the lower part of these rectangular structures, and hay was stored in the upper regions—the hay mows. A ramp or a convenient hillside allowed the farmer to haul hay directly into the hay mow.

Farmers learned that to increase milk production, cows had to be housed in a barn during the winter months. If their milking period was to extend beyond the summer pasturing months, they had to be fed stored feed. For many years, farmers had bragged about how little feed their cattle needed in winter. Some even boasted that the longer their cows were dry, the more milk they gave when they freshened in the spring. But experienced dairy farmers knew better. If you wanted your cows to give more milk, they had to milk longer than a few months in summer, and they had to be fed more than survival rations in the winter. Providing quality feed during the winter months was a challenge, however. Dried grass hay, even in sufficient quantity, simply lacked the nutritional value that enabled cows to maintain milk production. Enter the silo.

Silos

To some minds, the single most important influence on dairy milk production, and in turn, cheese production, was the silo. Wisconsin silos are, for the most part, upright, cylindrical structures. Chopped corn is blown into them and then allowed to ferment for a few weeks, until silage forms. Silage has a slightly acidic taste, is moist, and is relished by most cows.

Europeans were familiar with the fermentation process for turning green feed into silage by the 1870s. So were American farmers, but few paid much attention to it. Then in 1877, a Frenchman, August Goffart, published a book on silage making. After Goffart's book was translated into English in 1879, silos began appearing in Wisconsin.

One of the first silos constructed in the state was a trench silo, six feet wide, six feet deep, and thirty feet long, which Levi Gilbert of Fort Atkinson built in 1877. Dr. H. S. Weeks of Oconomowoc built a silo of stone and cement in 1880. Also in 1880, John Steele of Dodge County built a fieldstone silo that was twelve feet above ground and eleven feet below, for a total depth of twenty-three feet.

F. H. King of the University of Wisconsin's Agricultural Experiment Station had researched silos since the early 1880s. His major contribution was the wooden cylindrical silo, which had far fewer spoilage problems than the square silos that several farmers had constructed. The wooden stave silo, as it was later called, soon became the most popular silo on Wisconsin farms.

Farmers who built silos generally reported good results. Silage could be fed to cows throughout the winter months, and the cows milked more than those who merely ate grass hay. But not all farmers were convinced of the silo's benefits. The biggest prejudice against silage was the mistaken belief that it lowered the quality of milk. "Feed silage and lose your market," was the word heard from dairy farmers, especially those in Wisconsin. In some communities, creameries and cheese factories refused to accept milk from farmers who fed their cows silage.

Some agricultural publications were also skeptical. In its April 1881 issue, the *Farm Journal* editorialized:

> We shall not proclaim ensilage a humbug because that may not be the right word to describe it.... In this country many intelligent farmers, mostly of the fancy order, have become interested in it.... It is only a nine day's wonder. Practical farmers won't adopt it, except here and there, and in ten years from now the silos that are being built will be used for storing potatoes, turnips, beets, or ice.

But a few years later, the *Farm Journal* changed its position. It reported on silos constructed at the 1893 World's Fair in Chicago. Two silos had been erected, each thirty feet in diameter and thirty feet high, with a capacity of 300 tons each. "Progressive dairymen should not fail to examine this silo exhibit when they visit the fair," proclaimed a *Farm Journal* writer. Three years later, in 1899, the magazine printed instructions for building a round silo with a fieldstone foundation and wooden staves. But the adoption of silos on all dairy farms came slowly. In 1915, Hoard (of *Hoard's Dairyman*) was still arguing for silos and why farmers should build them.

The university's experiment station, with leadership from Professor F. H. King, promoted silos throughout the state. One staff person at the station proclaimed that the silo was "next to necessity in modern dairying." Slowly, the number of silos in the state increased, and then with the support of agricultural publications and promotion by the university, they began appearing everywhere.

By 1924 there were more than 100,000 silos in Wisconsin, and their numbers were increasing.[17] Silos appeared throughout rural areas. Spot a dairy barn and there was likely a silo nearby, at first one, then another. As the years passed more were added. Wisconsin soon became the largest silage producer in the United States (and still is). At first, silos were made of wood or fieldstone. Then poured concrete and concrete stave silos became popular. Still later, metal ones began appearing.

The silo, more than anything else, provided dairy cattle with something more to eat than dry grass hay during the long winter months. Later, research with forages would improve the hay crops as well.

In 1910, Wisconsin became the nation's leading cheese producer, pushing New York into second place.

Cheese Factory Numbers

In 1910, Wisconsin had 1,928 cheese factories; in 1918, there were 2,593 and in 1920, 2,771.[18] By 1920, only Iron and Oneida counties in the north and Pepin County, on the Mississippi River, had no cheese factories at all. Fourteen counties reported only one to four factories, but they were represented.

In 1920, the counties with the greatest number of cheese factories were Dodge (165), Green (151), Marathon (143), Iowa (135), Lafayette (130), Sheboygan (123), Manitowoc (120), Fond du Lac (116), and Shawano (101). These nine counties accounted for about half of the cheese factories in the state. Identify the counties with the greatest number of cheese factories, and you knew where the largest number of dairy farms and dairy cows were located.

17. Lampard, *The Rise of the Dairy Industry in Wisconsin*, 159-162.

18. "Number of Licensed Dairy Plants in Wisconsin, 1895-1942," Dairy Statistics Bulletin 200, Supplement No. 1, Wisconsin Crop Reporting Service (Madison, WI, 1942).

Easton Center Co-op Cheese Factory (W. F. Reetz, cheese maker), Ringle, Marathon County, c. 1920.

—From Wisconsin Cheese Makers Association.

Changes Occurring

The filled cheese episode of the 1880s had sent Wisconsin's cheese industry reeling. Without strong measures to punish the culprits, it is unlikely that Wisconsin would be known as the nation's dairyland today. But most of Wisconsin's cheese makers and farmers were committed to a quality product, and by the early 1900s, the popularity of Wisconsin's cheese was once again increasing. Between 1909 and 1911, Wisconsin cheese makers won the top three premiums in nearly every class of cheese judged at the Chicago and Milwaukee fairs, where they were in competition with cheese makers from throughout the United States and other countries.[19]

Cheese production was also increasing rapidly. By 1919, Wisconsin was producing more than sixty percent of all of the cheese made in the United States. As the population of the state, especially the southeastern regions, increased, the counties of Racine, Kenosha, Milwaukee, Walworth, Waukesha, and Jefferson began producing more milk for the nearby urban centers.[20] Cheese making was concentrated in south-central, southwestern, eastern and north-central Wisconsin.

Major changes occurred after 1900, both in the cheese factory and on the farm. Pasteurization of milk began on a commercial basis in 1913. Starting in 1916, Wisconsin cheese makers were required to have a license to make cheese. And by 1921 Wisconsin was the first state in the nation to institute mandatory grading for major cheese varieties.

19. Lampard, *The Rise of the Dairy Industry in Wisconsin*, 226.

20. Ibid., 268.

5 *Adjustment: 1920-1960*

Between 1920 and 1960, great changes took place in rural America. Trucks and cars replaced horses. Tractors began pulling plows. And electricity became available. In the cheese factory, electricity provided light, powered equipment, and ran refrigerators.

Changes in Cheese Factories

In 1922, the number of cheese factories in the state reached 2,807. Then numbers began declining. By 1924, there were 2,504 factories and in 1938, 1,917. Small plants closed or consolidated with neighboring plants.

But despite these closings, the 1920s and 1930s saw overall cheese production slowly edging upward. In 1920, the state produced 307.4 million pounds of cheese; in 1925, 362.7 million pounds were produced. Production declined to 310.4 million pounds in 1929, but by 1940, it had reached 406.9 million pounds.[1]

Cheese factories closed during these years for several reasons. Primary among them was the fact that trucks replaced horses and wagons. Milk could more easily be transported longer distances, and it was no longer necessary to have a cheese factory located nearby.

---

1. "Revisions in the Production of Creamery Butter, Cheese, and Ice Cream by States, 1910-1939" (Washington, D.C.: USDA Agricultural Marketing Service, December 1953) and "Production by States of All Manufactured Dairy Products, 1940" (Washington, D.C.: USDA, Bureau of Agricultural Economics, June 1942).

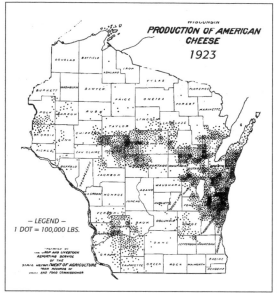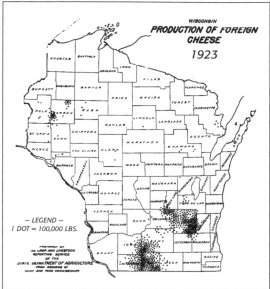

*Wisconsin produc-
tion of American
and foreign cheese,
1923.*

*—From the Biennial
Report of the Dairy and
Food Commissioner of
Wisconsin, 1924.*

Farmers had grown accustomed to hauling milk. Since the first cheese factory had opened, they had hauled milk with their horses each morning, after they finished milking. The short ride to the cheese factory—usually less than a couple miles—provided a respite from the morning's work and a chance for the farmer to inspect his neighbor's crops as he rode past with his team. Most farmers also enjoyed the opportunity to visit with their neighbors while they waited to unload their milk. To avoid spoilage in hot weather, farmers in some communities hauled their milk to the factories twice a day, after the morning and evening milkings. Factories made cheese in the morning and again in the evening after the last milk was delivered.

In several sections of the state, farmers hauled their milk to the factory in thirty-gallon milk cans (weighing more than 200 pounds each) that they lifted with tongs and a rope-and-pulley arrangement. Sometimes two men simply lifted the thirty-gallon cans onto a wagon. Many farmers, though, used ten-gallon milk cans that weighed about a hundred pounds when filled with milk. These cans were easier to handle, and could easily be slipped into the stock tank to cool.

There are many stories about farmers hauling their milk to the cheese plant. A popular one is about the farmer who stopped every day at a stream that was about halfway from his farm to the cheese factory. The farmer said he stopped there to rest his horses and give them a drink of water. One day when the cheese maker dumped the farmer's milk into the cheese factory receiving tank, a fish flopped out of the can with the milk.

"Don't know how that fish got there," the farmer said with a straight face. "Musta happened when I stopped to water the horses at the creek." The farmer wouldn't admit that while his horses were drinking, he was dumping stream water into the milk.

In another case, a farmer kept minnows in his water-filled cooling tank for ice fishing. One day, when the cheese maker dumped one of the farmer's milk cans, a four-inch minnow leaped into the milk tank.

"Nothing wrong with the minnow, either," the cheese maker said. "He just kept swimming around until we hauled him out. Didn't mind swimming around in milk one bit."

In the 1920s, cheese factories began buying trucks and sending them out to pick up milk from their farmer patrons. By doing this, the cheese factory eliminated the nagging problem of farmers coming in late with their milk, after the morning cheese-making process had already begun. (Some farmers bought their own trucks and continued to bring milk themselves, refusing to pay the small trucking costs that the cheese factories charged.)

With trucks that could travel faster and farther than a team and wagon, it was possible for a cheese factory to include patrons who were more than an easy horse and wagon trip away. There was no longer a need for a cheese factory to be located on nearly every country crossroads.

Milk trucks brought about another change as well. A new person became important in the cheese-making business—the milk hauler.

Patrons of the Monticello North Side Swiss Cheese Factory (Emil Escher and sons, cheese makers), 1934.
—*From Connie Halverson.*

Milk Haulers

With the invention of automobiles and trucks, new transportation arrangements had begun emerging. The January 1911 edition of the *Farm Journal* carried this advertisement for an "auto wagon," a cross between a truck and a car:

> An International Auto Wagon will earn its keep on your farm.
>
> It is in the seasons when your horses are all needed in the field or when the weather is most unfavorable for driving that the International Auto Wagon shows its real worth. It is always ready to take the milk or cream to the creamery, or take the children to school. With it you can oversee the farm, do all light hauling, visit any friend within thirty miles, take the family driving or to church.
>
> International Auto Wagons are sturdy, every-day workers. The frame, axles, and wheels are strong enough to carry any load the wagon should hold, over any road. The 20 HP engine has power enough to meet any road emergency. The transmission gives two forward speeds and reverse, without danger of stripping gears. The brakes are powerful.

About 85 percent of the milk produced in Wisconsin is made into cheese.

By the 1920s, trucks had improved considerably. One of the most popular was Henry Ford's Model T, designed to carry several cans of milk in the back.

By now, most of the cheese factories had switched to the popular ten-gallon cans. Many farmers learned how to cool their milk by placing milk cans in cattle-watering tanks or in specially designed cooling tanks. On many farms, water from the pump ran first to the milk-cooling tank and then to the stock-watering tank so no water was wasted. With farmers now able to keep their milk cool, it was only necessary for the milk hauler to pick up milk once a day.

Early milk trucks had open racks. As they traveled down country roads in summer, dust swirled around the cans and covered them with dirt—creating a challenging situation when the milk was dumped at the cheese factory. To keep out some of the dust, the racks were covered with canvas. By the 1950s, many milk trucks were entirely enclosed, solving the dust problem in a more permanent way.

The milk hauler's job was never easy. Winter was probably the

Loren Larson, left, and George Overby ready to unload milk cans at the Norden Cheese Factory, Town of Buffalo, Buffalo County, 1941.

—From Clifford T. Christenson.

worst time. Milk haulers became trailblazers on snow-drifted roads. A standard comment farmers made was, "If the milkman can make it through, then we probably can, too." Many days, however, the hauler became stuck and the entire load of milk froze, creating problems for the cheese maker when the milk finally arrived at the cheese factory.

Some milk haulers attached snowplows to the front of their trucks to help them negotiate the snow drifts. When the milk hauler had a snowplow, the farmer often depended on the driver to plow his driveway, an activity that slowed pickup time. Some farmers did not have time to shovel their driveways before the milk truck arrived; others just didn't do it. To make their rounds and get back to the cheese factory at a reasonable hour, milk haulers were on the road early in the morning.

Rodney Radloff of the Wild Rose Creamery recalled this incident about one of his milk haulers, who did not have a plow on his truck:

> Several farmers on our route wouldn't plow their driveways. I remember this incident clearly. It was a cold Saturday. The regular hauler's truck for the Westfield route had broken down. I drove the cheese factory's truck over there; the regular driver was along showing me the way. It was the middle of the afternoon when we got there. It had snowed the previous day and when we drove into yard, it wasn't plowed. We got about halfway up the drive and the truck went down. We were stuck.

"How many cans this farmer got?" I asked.

"Two," the regular driver answered.

"Just two. We drove in here and got stuck for two cans of milk."

The regular driver didn't reply.

"Doesn't this guy ever plow his driveway?" I asked.

"Nah, he never plows it."

"How do you get the milk?"

"I carry it out to the road."

"You're not gonna carry it tomorrow."

"Why not?"

"Because you're not; nobody's gonna carry milk out to the road."

It was a long driveway. Finally the farmer came home and saw the truck stuck in the middle of his driveway, in the deep snow.

"Don't you ever plow your driveway?" I asked.

The farmer didn't reply.

"You plow it today, or this driver isn't picking up your milk tomorrow."

Radloff said the next day the farmer had plowed his yard and he always had it plowed after that.

Next to winter, spring breakup was the next worst time for the milk hauler. Farm roads were not hard-surfaced so when the frost came out of the ground, roads became quagmires. Being stuck in snow was one thing; getting stuck in oozing mud was worse. At least the snow was clean.

Spring also brought flooded roads. Wilbur Witt, who hauled milk for the Amherst milk plant, liked telling this story. In the winter of 1950, he bought a new Ford truck, red with a cream-colored grill and a shiny white van into which the milk cans were placed. Witt had always driven used trucks, but now he had a new one and it was clear to everyone on the milk route he was proud of it. He claimed it would go almost anywhere.

The winter of 1950-51 had been a fierce one with more than average snow, and one bitter cold day after another. Witt's new Ford truck started every morning, no matter how cold, and he had yet to face a snow drift that he couldn't drive through. But one day in mid-March a southerly wind blew and the temperature shot up to forty-five degrees. Snow melted in a rush. With the ground still frozen, the meltwater gathered in the hollows and valleys, creating huge lakes where none had been before. Every low place on County A in Waushara County, one of Witt's regularly traveled routes, was immersed in water. This was not a problem for the new Ford milk truck. The clearance was high enough so he could drive through water without difficulty. He drove his new truck where no car could go.

Unfortunately, the day after the thaw, the wind switched to the northwest and the temperature plummeted below zero. Ponds were now covered with a thick layer of ice. So far, nothing had slowed Witt's new truck. It surely ought to handle a few ice-covered low places on the road. Indeed, he had been successful doing so until he came to the low place in County A between Mac Jenks' and Art Nordahl's farms.

What had worked before the ponds froze was to crank the truck up to about thirty miles per hour—not too slow, not too fast. Now the pond just before Nordahl's place came into view. It was larger than he remembered it and probably deeper, too. Its surface shone in the early morning sun. The front wheels of the truck rolled onto the ice and Witt thought that maybe the ice was thick enough to hold his vehicle. But when the weight of the entire truck was on the ice, Witt heard cracks and snaps and the truck broke through into about four feet of water and broken ice. He gunned

A milk truck used to pick up milk from farmers when milk was shipped in ten-gallon cans. Note the whey tanks in the background.

—*From Mrs. Irma Buelow.*

the engine, hoping that in icebreaker fashion he could bull his way through the ice-covered pond. It worked, for a few yards. Long enough for the ice to smash the grill on his new truck and cave in the red fenders. Long enough for the swirling ice water to reach the spark plugs in the engine and kill it. On that March day, Witt learned that even new Ford milk trucks were not invincible.

Here are more stories milk haulers like to tell:

Clifford Christenson started hauling milk for the Norden Cheese Factory, Town of Naples, Buffalo County, Wisconsin, in 1941. He was seventeen years old and drove a 1939 Mercury milk truck. The truck's flatbed held seventy-eight cans in thirteen rows, six cans to a row. During the peak season, Christenson double-decked the load to twelve cans in a row. He picked up milk from twenty-five patrons. Farmers living closest to the cheese factory hauled their own milk. Christenson hauled whey back to some of the farmers. His day started at 6 a.m. when he began loading whey at the cheese factory. His first pickup was at 7 a.m., and he had to be back to the factory with his full load of milk by 10 a.m. A filled can of milk weighed about 110 pounds, almost as much as Christenson weighed. Christenson recalled his first pickup was for Mrs. Endal and her daughter Agnes. They always invited him in for coffee, a special treat on a cold winter morning.

In 1921, Wisconsin became the first state in the nation to institute mandatory grading for major cheese varieties.

Every farmer had his own number and a designated place on the flatbed. Christenson remembers many of the numbers. Mrs. Endal's was #6, Joe Berg's, #15, Art Kins', #27, and Melvin Strommen's, #31.

At the cheese factory, Albert Engen would bring gas for the trucks. Christenson remembers that Engen always arrived when the cheese was in curds. Engen would take a big scoop of curds out of the vat, sit on the intake steps, and eat them. When sweet corn was in season, the crew at the cheese factory roasted ears on the hot coals in the cheese factory boiler. The Norden Cheese Factory closed in 1944 and the building became a home.

Robert Gerber started hauling milk in December 1949, when some farmers still cooled their milk in stock tanks because few had milk houses. He also recalls that farmers milked few cows during the winter months.

"With me starting out in December, I almost starved to death. One farmer would have a can and a half. Another would have two cans. The cans were often cooling in water, which was frozen, and

I'd have to chop loose the cans before I could load them. We really had a rough time," Gerber said.

By the mid-1950s, farmers producing Grade A milk (that is, milk meeting the highest quality standards) began buying refrigerated bulk tanks to store and cool their milk. Gerber recalls the time when the milk plant to which he was hauling milk decided to switch to bulk milk and do away with the ten-gallon milk cans.

"We had a meeting with the farmers and they were all for it. There was a good incentive. The milk plant paid a twenty cents per hundred pounds premium to a farmer who switched to bulk. I had six trucks at the time for cans, and with the switch to bulk, I only needed two bulk trucks."

When Gerber discovered he didn't need as many trucks on the road for bulk-milk systems, he decided to sell bulk tanks to help pay for his new tank trucks. He became a dealer for a Missouri company that manufactured the tanks. At first, they were not easy to sell. They cost $2,000 and more. Farmers had used ten-gallon milk cans for years, and some were skeptical about changing to a fancy bulk tank. The premiums the milk plants paid for milk cooled in bulk tanks helped farmers change their minds. So did the loans made available by the Production Credit Association (PCA) with no money down.

One of the claims bulk-cooler salesmen made was that the farmer would get more total milk when using a bulk cooler because some milk sticks to the sides of the old milk cans and is lost. There was some truth to that.

Gerber remembers selling a bulk cooler to a fellow near Hollandale. "I went back a couple of weeks later to see how it was going," he said.

The farmer looked Gerber in the eye and said, "You told me I would get more milk by putting in this bulk-milk cooler, but I'm getting less."

"What happened, Joe?" Gerber asked.

The farmer began laughing. "I've got nine kids and my kids like the cold milk so good they're drinking twice as much as before."

Many farmers complained about their new bulk-milk coolers. One of the biggest complaints came from farmers who said they couldn't skim off cream for their breakfast cereal. The bulk tank agitates the milk, and thus there is little cream that accumulates on the top.

One farmer switched from a water-bath can milk cooler to a bulk tank and complained he couldn't cool his beer with his new bulk cooler. With his old system, he had cool beer year-round.[2]

Now milk hauling has changed dramatically, with farmer-owned teams and wagons replaced by shiny stainless-steel tanker trucks traveling the country roads. Where once farmers lived within a mile or two of a cheese factory, now some may live fifty or more miles away. With improvements in milk trucks came improvements in country roads. At one time, the vast majority of roads were dirt or gravel; today most are hard-surfaced, allowing the tanker trucks to make their rounds quite easily. It could be said that milk trucks are responsible for Wisconsin's good rural road system. Winter continues to be a challenge, so does spring break-up when even hard-surfaced roads pose problems. But nothing today compares to the spring mud of a dirt or gravel road.

Cheese Factory Numbers Continue Declining

In 1940, just before World War II, there were 1,880 cheese factories operating in Wisconsin. In 1950, five years after the war's end, the number of Wisconsin cheese factories had dropped to 1,279.[3]

---

2. From a 1995 videotaped interview, on file with the Historic Cheesemaking Center, Monroe, WI.

3. "Number of Licensed Dairy Plants in Wisconsin, 1895-1942," Wisconsin Crop Reporting Service, and *Wisconsin 1996 Dairy Facts*.

Many of the operating cheese factories were still relatively small, serving farmers in their local community. One such factory was the Bud Cheese Factory in Vernon County, operated by Floyd Burt. He received his cheese maker's license in 1935 and started working in a factory that had no electricity. Cheese makers in those days often worked twelve hours a day, seven days a week. The farmers' milk was made into cheese the same day it was received because there was no way to cool and store it. Nevertheless, as Burt said, "It was up to the cheese maker to make a quality product or it would not sell. We always stressed quality cheese rather than quantity."

Burt operated the Bud Cheese Factory for more than forty-six years and has related many stories. "There were lots of worries in the cheese-making business," he recalled. "Farmers were always shopping for a better market for their milk. We had lots of competition so I tried to get a good market for my cheese so I could pay farmers a good price."

Burt remembered the time when his milk truck broke down.

As you know, whey is the by-product of cheese making and if not handled properly, it goes sour and ferments. We were still hauling milk in milk cans and taking whey back to farmers so they could feed it to their pigs. It was summer time. Hot. The truck had stopped and we couldn't get parts

The interior of the Wolf River Cheese Factory, Shawano County, c. 1920. The factory was owned by area farmers and operated by Hugo Raddant, far left.

—From Mrs. Harry Buelow.

until the next day. The whey tank on the truck was full, and it was standing out in the sun. A farmer asked if he could haul the whey to his pigs—there were several hundred pounds of it.

It was a hot day and the thirsty pigs drank a lot of the whey. In thirty minutes or so, the pigs began squealing and staggering around the yard and then falling over. The farmer called me at the cheese factory.

"The whey has killed my pigs," the farmer said. Well I hurried right down to his farm and when I got there, the farmer was standing by his hog pen with the "dead pigs."

"Whey does not kill pigs," I said. The farmer didn't believe it. We waited. In a few hours the pigs were all up and running around. They had gotten drunk from drinking too much fermented whey. Both the farmer and I were very relieved.

Changes on the Farm

Between 1930 and 1960, per capita cheese consumption in the U.S. increased 100 percent while the population increased fifty percent.

Changes were occurring on farms as well as in the cheese factories. Electricity had come to many farms by 1941. With electricity, milking machines became popular, and the size of the dairy herds increased. Milking ten or twelve cows by hand had been about all one man could handle. Even with a couple of husky children, milking twenty cows by hand had been the upper limit. But with a milking machine, one man could easily milk twenty or thirty cows by himself.

In 1925, there were about 1.9 million milk cows in Wisconsin. In 1945, there were 2.36 million. This was the peak year for dairy cows before the numbers starting dropping. By 1960, there were only 2.15 million dairy cows in the state.

Wisconsin boasted 168,890 dairy farms in 1929. By 1939 the number had dropped to 160,124. In 1950 the number slid to 143,000, and in 1960 dairy farm numbers reached 105,000, with nothing but further decline anticipated.[4]

Thirty-eight thousand farmers quit farming during the 1950s. On average, 3,800 farms went out of business each year during that decade, an average of ten farms a day. Farm boys and girls, upon completing high school, moved off the land. Some went to

4. *Wisconsin 1996 Dairy Facts*, and U. S. Census of Agriculture for 1929 and 1939.

Milk can washer. Nearly every cheese factory accepted milk from farmers in ten-gallon milk cans, which were washed after they were emptied. Fairview Cheese Factory, Shawano County.

—From Mrs. Irma Buelow.

college, but most took jobs in the state's cities and towns. Many longed to return to the farm, but the vast majority of them never did, except perhaps when they retired from a city job and bought a few acres in the country and became hobby farmers.

Their parents stayed on the farm, milked a few cows and eked out a living as dairy herds became larger, and farm investments skyrocketed. When these farmers became too old to work the land, they sold their farms.

Through better feeding, especially improved winter feeding, individual cow milk production steadily increased. In 1925, average milk production per cow was 5,410 pounds; by 1950, cows were averaging 6,850 pounds, and by 1960, 8,270 pounds. The increases in milk production were important. For too long dairy farmers had assumed that a cow could only give so much milk and that nothing the farmer did would increase production.[5]

By 1939 the first artificial dairy-cattle breeding cooperatives were established in Rock, Langlade, and Barron counties. Although relatively slow to catch on, artificial breeding of dairy cows had great advantages for the dairy farmer. No longer did he have to contend with a temperamental bull that sometimes turned on its owner. Moreover, the best bulls in the region were available to the farmer. By 1941, artificial insemination was on its way, and the genetics of Wisconsin's dairy cattle began a slow and steady improvement, with corresponding increases in milk production.

Other changes occurred as well. Tractors on the farm meant

---

5. "Milk Cows and Production of Milk and Milkfat: Wisconsin, Selected Years," *Wisconsin 1996 Dairy Facts.*

The Opie Factory was an old-fashioned Swiss cheese factory located on Highway 78, four miles south of Gratiot in Lafayette County. Pictured are John Bussman Sr. (left) and Delbert Colbeck in 1938.

—From Tammy Opie.

more acres could be worked in less time. In 1927, University of Wisconsin College of Agriculture engineers developed a field forage harvester that made harvesting corn for silage far less the backbreaking job it had been. Silos became even more popular.

After World War II, mechanization beyond anything anyone could have imagined came to the farm. Electricity had first arrived because of the Rural Electrification Administration (REA) program. Electric cooperatives assumed farmers wanted electric lights. They did. But they soon demanded more than light bulbs to replace kerosene lanterns in the barn. They wanted an electric motor in the pump house to pump water, and another electric motor to run their milking machine. They wanted a motor-operated barn cleaner to remove cow manure from the gutters in the barn. They wanted a silo unloader so they didn't have to fork silage by hand from a tower silo. Farmers soon had electric saws, electric welders, and a host of other electrically powered tools and equipment.

Toward Higher Quality Cheese

Cheese makers had long known that quality milk is necessary for quality cheese. But some Wisconsin dairy farmers didn't get the message. With milking machines, the farmer's job was easier, but in many instances the cheese maker's job became more difficult. Harry Raisleger, a longtime Kewaunee County cheese maker, recalled, "Some farmers didn't know how to clean their milking machines properly. As a result I had many problems making cheese. Many times I stayed up until nine or ten at night to get enough lactic acid in the cheese to overcome the gas that resulted from dirty milk. One time the cheese was so gassy it rolled right off the shelf. To correct the problem, I heated water in milk cans, drove out to a farm, and cleaned the farmer's milking machine for him. I was trying to teach him how to care for it properly."

Raisleger recalled another time when a farmer delivered bad milk. "I took two quarts of his milk, put rennet in it, and tried to make cheese from it. It came out fluffy, gassy, and smelled bad. Normally, the curd would be a solid pad on the bottom of the jar. The next morning when the farmer came in, I showed him the product from his milk. I asked him if he would want to eat cheese like that. He smelled it, said 'sure,' and ate it. My theory didn't work. Anyway, I went out to his farm, too, and helped him clean up his milking machine and other equipment."

By 1950, Wisconsin farmers were required to have milk houses, buildings that may be attached to the barn but were separated from it with a wall. County agricultural agents of the College of Agriculture, in cooperation with dairy plants, launched a massive educational effort that resulted in milk of increasingly higher quality. Wisconsin became known for its quality dairy products, especially its cheese.

Mozzarella cheese production soared after World War II. Veterans had acquired a taste for a food they had eaten in Italy—pizza.

The demand for cheese continued to grow, and Wisconsin cheese factories tried to meet it. In 1950, Wisconsin produced nearly 558 million pounds of cheese, and by 1960 production increased to 641 million pounds.[6]

Pizza Cheeses

Italian cheeses, such as Asiago, Parmesan, provolone, Romano, and mozzarella, had long been considered "foreign" cheeses, along with Swiss, Limburger, and a few others. In 1950, only twenty-five percent of Wisconsin's cheese was of this type. But starting that year, something developed that no one expected—pizza pie, as it was called in those days. What was pizza pie? Was it like apple pie, or maybe custard pie? Those who knew chuckled, for pizza pie and apple pie are about as similar as hard water and ice.

Who brought pizza pie to the United States? The usual answer is that American servicemen who fought in Italy during World War II were introduced to pizza and learned how to make it.

---

6. *Wisconsin 1996 Dairy Facts.*

Perhaps most important, they brought back with them a taste for this somewhat spicy, strange food, which includes a mixture of tomato, cheese, and sausage, and sometimes anchovies, peppers, and other ingredients, all resting on a thin crust.

In the mid-1950s, pizza became a popular "teen-ager food," and when the teenagers married, they continued eating pizza, by the hundreds of thousands. To meet the demand for pizza cheese, cheese factories began switching from cheddar to mozzarella, or they began making both kinds of cheeses.

Aids to Dairy Farmers

When the first countywide Dairy Herd Improvement Association (DHIA) was established in Winnebago County in 1941, an important management tool for farmers emerged. With the assistance of the College of Agriculture's Dairy Science Department, Dairy Herd Improvement Associations spread throughout the state. DHIA field men collected samples of milk from dairy farmers who enrolled for the service and recorded the amount of milk each cow gave. At a regional laboratory, the milk was tested for its butterfat level and the results were mailed to the farmer. With this information, farmers learned which of their cows were producing well and which were freeloaders. By 1952, computer processing was added to the Dairy Herd Improvement work at the College of Agriculture, and farmers began receiving computer printouts about each of their cows.

Farmers were also greatly aided by a breakthrough in the treatment of brucellosis. Brucellosis, also known as Bang's disease, is a dairy cow disease that results in aborted calves. By the late 1940s it had become so severe that some fifteen percent of Wisconsin's herds were infected. It was a dangerous disease for humans as well, resulting in undulant fever that was not fatal but considerably debilitating. Farmers with infected cattle were often the first to come down with the disease. Veterinary researchers at the University of Wisconsin developed improved methods of detecting the disease and a vaccine to prevent it. Within five years, the incidence of brucellosis was reduced to less than 0.1 percent of Wisconsin dairy herds.

All in all, the year 1960 marked the end of four decades of profound changes in dairy farming and cheese making. However, more changes were to come.

6 *Transition: 1960-Present*

From the 1960s to the present, cheese factory production has continued to increase. In 1960, Wisconsin cheese plants produced 641 million pounds of cheese. By 1980, yearly cheese production had climbed to nearly 1.5 billion pounds. In 1990, it was 1.9 billion pounds, and in 1995 it had reached 2.09 billion pounds and was still climbing. Dairy farm and cheese factory numbers, on the other hand, have declined.[1]

Cheese Factory Changes

Wisconsin had 798 cheese factories in 1960, 481 in 1970, 334 in 1980, and only 142 in 1995. In the thirty-five years between 1960 and 1995, 656 cheese factories closed. Some factories bought out their neighbors and expanded. Others merely shut down, and the buildings became homes or were used for other purposes.

Why did so many cheese factories close? John Umhoefer, executive director of the Wisconsin Cheese Makers Association, interpreted the situation this way:

It used to be the owner was the cheese maker, he was the salesman, and he was a one-person show. Cheese making went from being something that you did to sustain yourself and maybe a few neighbors, to a business that sells products

---

1. Data cited in this chapter on cheese factories and milk production from *Wisconsin 1996 Dairy Facts.*

to New York and Florida. When cheese makers started out, they were processing milk for four people, and they probably sold their cheese within fifty miles. Today about ninety-five percent of Wisconsin's cheese is sold outside the state.

With the switch to bulk trucks, the milk hauler pumped the milk directly from the farmer's refrigerated bulk tank to the bulk truck and then drove on to the cheese factory. Once there, the milk was pumped into holding tanks. There were no ten-gallon milk cans to dump and no cans to wash. Can-washing machines had often been temperamental, slowing the loading of empty cans and in turn delaying the unloading of full cans from the trucks. Now, with refrigerated milk-holding tanks (which usually looked like silos to passers-by), cheese makers had some control over when they made cheese. No longer was cheese making a seven-days-a-week occupation. The cheese factory could close on Sundays.

Changes on the Farm

Not only did cheese factory numbers continue declining, so did dairy farm numbers. In 1950, Wisconsin had 143,000 dairy farms. By 1970 the number had dropped to 64,000, a decline of 79,000 farms in twenty years. The Wisconsin landscape was changing dramatically too. Small towns, which depended on dairy farmers to buy tractors, trucks, feed, and animal supplies, felt the pinch. Grist mills, some of them a hundred years old and more, quit grinding cattle feed. Implement dealers closed down. So did hardware and fertilizer stores.

The decline persisted. In 1980, Wisconsin had 45,000 dairy farms; in 1990, 34,000; and in 1995, 28,000. Some people began asking if the family farm, the cornerstone of dairy farming in Wisconsin for so many years, had become a piece of Wisconsin's past. In forty-five years, Wisconsin lost 115,000 dairy farms.

Agricultural economists tried to explain what was happening. They said market forces were at work, and to become more efficient the small family farm had to either grow larger or close down. Many family farmers had no means to enlarge. They feared adding to their debt. They saw neighbors borrow huge sums of money and lose everything when milk prices declined, drought cut into feed supplies, or illness struck down the farmer.

Dairy cow numbers also decreased. In 1950, Wisconsin had

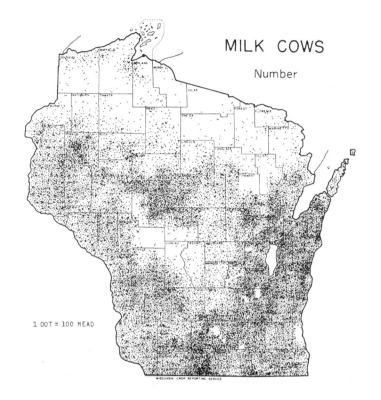

MILK COWS

Number

1 DOT = 100 HEAD

Milk cows in Wisconsin, 1963.

—From the Directory of Wisconsin Dairy Plants, Wisconsin Department of Agriculture.

2.16 million milk cows; in 1970, 1.8 million. The number of cows in Wisconsin decreased by 360,000 in twenty years.

In 1980, the number of cows seemed to be stabilizing at 1.8 million head, but then the downward slide continued. In 1990, Wisconsin had 1.7 million cows, and by 1995 the number had dropped to less than 1.5 million. Some began to wonder if Wisconsin would hang onto its title as "America's Dairyland," especially with the number of milk cows increasing in Texas, Arizona, Washington, Idaho, and, especially, California, where the size of a dairy cow herd often numbered in the thousands. In 1950, the average Wisconsin dairy farm had only fifteen milk cows; by 1970 it had twenty-eight. By the middle 1990s, the average Wisconsin herd size had increased to fifty-two. Some Wisconsin farmers milked more than five or six hundred cows, though these were few.

Something else was changing in the Wisconsin countryside. In 1950, it was common to see Guernseys, Ayrshires, Brown Swiss, and Jersey cows grazing in Wisconsin pastures, along with Holsteins. But slowly the black and white Holstein cow replaced the other breeds in the cow yards. There were still small numbers of the other breeds; some dairymen simply couldn't see switching to those ever-hungry Holsteins, which demanded larger stalls in the barn and stronger fences when they were outside. But without question, the Holstein cow produced more milk than cows of other breeds. True, the fat content of Holstein milk was considerably lower than Jersey and Guernsey milk, but volume won out over fat content. Most dairy farmers wanted a milk cow that would produce lots of milk, and the Holstein fit the bill. By the 1980s, more than ninety percent of the milk cows in Wisconsin were Holsteins.

Dairy farmers, because of artificial insemination, better feeding programs, and better management, began seeing substantial increases in the production of milk per cow. In 1960, average per-cow production was 8,270 pounds of milk a year; in 1970, average per-cow production increased to 10,163 pounds. In all, Wisconsin produced about 14.8 billion pounds of milk in 1950; by 1970, with considerably fewer cows, the state produced 18.4 billion pounds of milk. By 1985, the state's milk production had climbed to 24.7 billion pounds. Then it began a decline. In 1995, total milk production was 22.9 billion pounds and somewhat stabilized.

In 1993, California edged ahead of Wisconsin in total milk production. In 1995, California produced 25.3 billion pounds of milk compared with Wisconsin's 22.9 billion pounds.[2] What Wisconsin dairy people thought would never happen, happened. California became the leading milk-producing state in the nation.

Milking cows got easier when farmers installed bulk tanks in their milk houses and replaced the ten-gallon milk cans that had been a fixture in the dairy industry since the 1800s. Farmers also installed pipelines in their barns so the milk from each cow flowed directly to the bulk tank. This setup was cleaner and more convenient, and the farmer did not have to lift and pour every quart of milk his cows produced. By the 1960s, the milk can had all but disappeared. Before long they reappeared, but this time as objects collected by antique buyers.

In the 1960s, farmers began installing milking parlors. These were milking rooms attached to the barn; the cows walked through them to be milked. Milking parlors made milking even

---

2. "Whey to go, Wis! Cheese hits record," *The Capital Times*, May 4-5, 1996.

easier. In most, the farmer stood at a level lower than the cows. That meant he could stand rather than stoop while attaching and removing the milking machines to and from each cow.

But even though backbreaking manual labor was replaced with machines, the farmer had to contend with keeping all these machines operating—and figuring out a way to pay for them.

Corn silage remained a popular feed, and farmers continued to build silos. Some dairy farmers had three, four, five, even six or more silos. With new forage equipment that could cut alfalfa and other forage crops into short lengths and blow it into a wagon, farmers began making silage from hay crops. Haylage it was called. For years, however, some farmers would have nothing to do with it. They said it was bad for their cows, difficult to feed, and smelly to handle. Moreover, they said, the cows didn't like it. But slowly haylage caught on, and now dairy farmers had both corn and grass silage, as the latter was sometimes called, to feed their cattle through the long winter months.

Cheese Consumption

Cheddar cheese has always been America's favorite cheese. But as time went on, consumers began enjoying a host of other cheeses: blue cheese, Gouda, Edam, Havarti, Asiago, mozzarella,

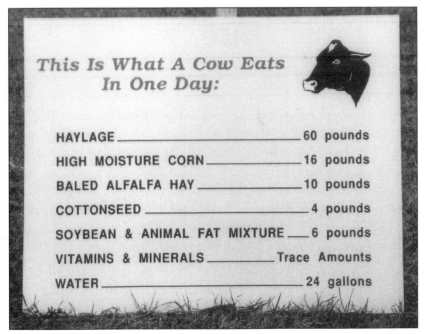

This Is What A Cow Eats In One Day:

HAYLAGE	60 pounds
HIGH MOISTURE CORN	16 pounds
BALED ALFALFA HAY	10 pounds
COTTONSEED	4 pounds
SOYBEAN & ANIMAL FAT MIXTURE	6 pounds
VITAMINS & MINERALS	Trace Amounts
WATER	24 gallons

A dairy cow converts huge amounts of feed and water into milk. Haylage is silage made from grasses and legumes and stored in silos.

*Wisconsin cheese
production:*

*1920-
307.4 million pounds
1940-
406.9 million pounds
1960-
641 million pounds
1980-
1.5 billion pounds
1995-
2.09 billion pounds*

muenster, Monterey Jack, Colby and Swiss, for example.

By 1995, the annual consumption of cheese had risen to nearly twenty-eight pounds per person. About one-third of the cheese was sold through retail outlets, one-third to food-service vendors, and one-third to food-manufacturing markets. Cheddar and Italian cheese experienced the greatest growth. Since 1980, the consumption of cheddar cheese has increased one-third, to about nine pounds per person. Consumption of Italian cheese (including mozzarella) has more than doubled during this period. Consumption of mozzarella—the primary cheese on pizza—increased from 2.2 pounds per person in 1980 to more than ten pounds in 1995. Mozzarella production increased from 144 million pounds in 1975, to 559.9 million pounds in 1990, and to 633.4 million pounds in 1995. Mozzarella cheese has become the second most popular cheese made in Wisconsin, after cheddar.

Fast-food pizza chains such as Domino's and Pizza Hut account for some of the increase in cheese consumption. Not to be overlooked are other fast-food restaurants, such as McDonald's, Hardees, Arby's, and Wendy's, which serve cheeseburgers and other foods with cheese as an ingredient. Restaurants featuring Mexican food, such as tacos and enchiladas, are also strong cheese markets.[3]

Whey

Two products result from cheese making: curds and whey. Curds become cheese. Whey becomes a problem. At least that was the case for many years. In the early days of cheese factories, farmers brought their milk to the cheese factory and took home whey. They fed whey to their pigs, who relished it and grew rapidly on it. As farmers produced more milk and quit raising pigs, they didn't want the whey. Sometimes the whey was spread on farmers' fields to get rid of it. Drive by an older cheese factory, and invariably you will spot the whey tank outside. Every cheese factory had one. One cheese maker's son (who shall remain anonymous) delivered whey to farmers at night, and what the farmers couldn't use he dumped alongside the road just to get rid of it.

As the years passed, problems with whey disposal increased. University researchers looked for alternative uses for this cursed

---

3. "Pizza Propels Cheese Consumption Climb," *Agri-View*, May 23-24, 1996.

Kiefer Brothers Creamery, Columbia County, 1996. A former cheese factory located five miles north of Pardeeville on Highway 22.

by-product of the cheese industry. Drying whey was one approach. Dried whey consists of about seventy-five percent lactose, thirteen percent protein, and a few minor ingredients. With additional filtration, the protein of dried whey can be increased to as much as eighty percent.

The food industry discovered that dried whey, combined with some other products, could replace eggs in bakery glazes. The whey mixture is sprayed on bakery goods to better hold such toppings as sesame seeds, poppy seeds, and crushed grains. This filtrated and dried whey, known as whey protein concentrate, is also used in sponge cakes, muffins, and white layer cakes. It is also used in low-fat soups to provide a rich creamy taste and appearance.[4] Ethanol (a form of alcohol), which is blended with gasoline to provide an alternative energy source, also can be made from whey. A commercial whey ethanol plant in Plover is in a redesigned corn-based ethanol factory that failed in the early 1980s. Protein is separated from the whey and the remaining sugar-water solution provides the main ingredient for ethanol, which is made at this combination brewery and distillery.

Changes in the Wisconsin Cheese Makers Association

The Wisconsin Cheese Makers Association (WCMA), organized in 1893, continues to be an important force in the cheese industry. A major function of the association, which has its offices

---

4. "New Uses for Dairy Products Not So Whey-Out," *Agri-View*, May 23-24, 1996.

Wilbert Strahm, Jac. Voegeli, Walter Zeller, Conrad Stauffacher, and Wilbert Dick, directors of the Monticello North Side Swiss Cheese Factory in Green County, sharing some Swiss cheese in 1948.

—From Connie Halverson.

in downtown Madison, is to keep an eye on state government, especially those branches advocating various kinds of regulations affecting the cheese industry. As John Umhoefer, the current executive director, said, "The Wisconsin Cheese Makers Association is a lobbying association to assure a good business climate [for the cheese industry]." The association also closely watches national regulations and legislation affecting the cheese industry.

In the early years, the association's mission was to help individual cheese makers. It provided educational opportunities and sought to improve the quality of Wisconsin cheese. It also served as a social organization for cheese makers and their spouses. Annual meetings were, as Umhoefer described them, "a yearly outing for the cheese maker—with a plea that he should come to Milwaukee and take a couple days off with his wife."

Today, cheese-making companies are the focus of the WCMA. Seventy-seven companies belong and represent about a hundred operating plants. Umhoefer used the Stella Foods as an example of how WCMA membership works today. "Stella has about nine

plants in the state, so they send us a flat fee and all nine of their plant managers and all their cheese makers are members. When a company joins, everyone who works for them has joined."

WCMA continues to sponsor educational events, seminars, workshops, and conferences. They hold an equipment exposition in even-numbered years that attracts about 1,500 participants. Topics discussed at a recent annual meeting held in La Crosse included "Cheese Export Opportunities," "Your Cheese Label as Marketing Tool," "Maximizing Cheese Yield," and "Twenty-first Century Policy and Regulation." In odd-numbered years the association sponsors a technical seminar that draws nearly a thousand people. A recent one held in Green Bay offered seminars on everything from lower-fat cheese to maintaining cheese quality.

Since the late 1800s, WCMA has sponsored cheese contests to promote excellence in cheese making. That tradition continues today. The 1996 International Cheese-Judging Contest attracted more than 800 entries in twenty classes. An international panel of ten judges evaluated the entries and made decisions. In addition to Wisconsin cheese makers, who won sixteen awards, winners were from Canada, New Zealand, Ireland, Denmark, the Netherlands, Finland, France, Australia, Spain, Switzerland, and Sweden. Other states with winners included California, Michigan, Ohio, Missouri, Utah, Pennsylvania, and New Jersey. The World Championship contest is held in even-numbered years, and the United States Championship Cheese Contest in odd-numbered years.

Center for Dairy Research

Established at the University of Wisconsin-Madison in 1986, the Center for Dairy Research is funded primarily with money received from the Wisconsin Milk Marketing Board. Additional funding sources include the National Milk Marketing Board (Dairy Management, Inc.) and private industry.

The center has two major functions: conducting research on dairy topics and communicating that research to those who have the most use for it—dairy plants, cheese makers, and dairy farmers. The research program has concentrated on the demand for and uses of milk fat, new applications for nonfat milk components, cheese technology, and dairy food safety and quality.

Norman Olson, director of the center for several years, said the center has "reinvigorated research for dairy products, especially

76704

Wisconsin State

DEPARTMENT OF AGRICULTURE

MADISON

This is to certify that ALVIN X. BUKOLZER

of MONROE, WISCONSIN under authority of

Section 97.03 of the Wisconsin Statutes is hereby licensed to

Engage in the MANUFACTURE of CHEESE as a CHEESEMAKER

until December 31, subject to revocation or renewal, as provided by law
1943

In witness whereof, we hereunto set our hand and official seal this 29th *day of* November 19 43

STATE DEPARTMENT OF AGRICULTURE

Milton H. Button

DIRECTOR

THIS LICENSE NOT TRANSFERABLE

Photocopy of the cheese maker's license that Alvin X. Bukolzer received in 1943, after attending a cheese-makers school. He renewed his license each year for fifty-one years.

—From Historic Cheesemaking Center.

cheese." Some of its accomplishments include the development of a Wisconsin-style Havarti cheese, reduced-fat cheddar, and a type of mozzarella that is easier to make. The center also searches for new ways of using milk fat (especially in the food industry) and whey.

Another emphasis of the center has been the improvement of cheese quality. A few years ago, a common problem with some cheddar and Colby cheeses was the formation of white spots that showed up after the cheese was in the market case at the grocery store. The spots were calcium lactate, not mold as many people thought, but their appearance detracted from sales. Researchers figured out a way to correct the problem; as a result the cheese industry saved $6 million in sales annually.

The Dairy Research Center also provides consultation directly to cheese companies. The cheese company pays for the service. These connections have resulted in the development of new products and a host of other benefits for the industry.

In addition, the center jointly sponsors short courses with University Extension specialists. A recent schedule included "Whey and Whey Utilization Short Course," "Polish Cheese Artisan Course," "Dairy Plant Water and Waste Management Short Course," "Applied Cheese-Grading Short Course,"

"Wisconsin Cheese-Grading Short Course," and a "Wisconsin Cheese Technology" short course.

The Wisconsin Center for Dairy Research and the Wisconsin Milk Marketing Board sponsor a "Master Cheese Maker" program. To enter the program, applicants must have had their cheese maker's licenses for at least ten years and must have a special interest in becoming masters of their trade. The program is two years long (on a part-time basis) and combines old European cheese-making traditions with new ways of doing things. The first class of four master cheese makers graduated in 1997 and included Doug Peterson, Foremost Farms, Arena; Terry Lensmire, Land O' Lakes, Kiel; Randy Krahenbuhl, Prima Käse, Monticello; and Tom Jenny, Old Wisconsin Cheese, Platteville.

The University of Wisconsin Dairy Short Course was initiated in 1889. It helps cheese and butter makers improve their skills and has provided training for thousands of Wisconsin cheese makers.

The Future

If the past is any indicator of future direction, then great changes will continue in the dairy industry, on the farm and in the processing plants.

Dairy Farms

How does the future look for the dairy farmer? Gerald (Jerry) Kronschnabel, who is with the Germania Dairy Automation Division of Alfa-Lavel (a large dairy equipment company that sells modern milking equipment to farmers) has some ideas.

> I see four things occurring. First, dairy farming will continue to switch from a way of life to a business. Second, dairy cow management must catch up with genetics. Cows are bred for high production, but they must be fed properly or that high production potential will not be realized. Third, the size of dairy herds will continue to increase. We'll see more and more herds with upwards of 200 milking cows. The largest herds now in the Midwest are around a thousand cows. And fourth, specialization. We'll see fewer dairy farmers but they will focus all their attention on their cows. Someone else will take care of the field work.

Dairy farmers themselves seem divided on which way to head into the future. Some are buying cows and increasing their herds as rapidly as they can, aiming toward 500 or more milking cows.

Neal Jorgensen, dean of the College of Agricultural and Life Sciences at the University of Wisconsin, predicts that dairy herds will grow larger and milk production per cow will continue to increase. "The average number of cows per herd will go to about a hundred in the next five years, from about sixty right now," he said. "But I don't think we're going to see many herds above 750. It's too difficult to handle the waste."

Jorgensen shared some details about a large dairy farm operation in southwestern Wisconsin. "This dairyman milks 650 cows. His crew milks them three times a day, and there is only one person in the milking parlor at a time. He has a milking parlor system in which sixteen cows are milked at the same time. All that person does is prepare the cow and put on the machine. Everything else is automatic. The cow is identified. The milk flow is automatic; the teat cups are taken off automatically, and the gate swings up and the cows go out automatically. An operator milks about 115 cows an hour."

Other dairy farmers are less sure that this is the way to go—especially when it means assuming a huge debt load. Organic farmers believe they can make a fair living from a smaller number of cows by following organic farming principles and selling their milk at a premium.

American cheese plants in Wisconsin, 1963.

—From the Directory of Wisconsin Dairy Plants, Wisconsin Department of Agriculture.

AMERICAN CHEESE PLANTS

1963

I Dot = I Plant

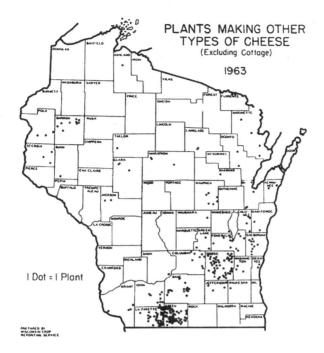

PLANTS MAKING OTHER
TYPES OF CHEESE
(Excluding Cottage)

1963

I Dot = I Plant

*Plants making
other than American
cheese in Wisconsin,
1963.*

*—From the Directory of
Wisconsin Dairy Plants,
Wisconsin Department
of Agriculture.*

Some farmers believe that rather than trying to constantly increase the amount of milk produced per cow with highly mechanized and often costly feeding systems, cows should be allowed to graze in carefully managed pastures. These farmers believe that they can increase net income on their dairy farms by lowering production costs, rather than trying to increase individual cow output. Grazing networks—that is, farmers willing to help other farmers establish profitable grazing systems—exist throughout the state. In January 1997, twenty-two such networks were listed in a weekly farm paper.

Other farmers—somewhat older—have little, if any, debt. Their herds consist of about fifty milking cows. These farmers will continue to operate as they have in the past until they retire. After retirement, their kind of dairy operation will probably not continue. Whoever purchases their farm will likely follow one of the three options outlined above.

Cheese Factories

Cheese factories operating in Wisconsin today are either very large or they are specialized plants whose products appeal to niche markets. The future for the mid-size cheese factory is a bit cloudy. Presently, the largest cheese operation in Wisconsin is

Foremost Farms, which has about 5,000 producers in the state. Foremost Farms consolidated with Golden Guernsey Dairy Cooperative and Morning Glory Farms in the mid-1990s. Headquartered in Baraboo, it has members in Minnesota, Iowa, Illinois, Michigan, and Ohio, as well as Wisconsin. Foremost's major cheese product is bulk cheddar, which it sells to major food companies such as Kraft, Schreiber Foods, and Sargento. Sales in 1995 were $1.4 billion.[5]

Other large cheese producers in Wisconsin are AMPI, which has 2,000 farmer producers; Stella Foods, which has 1,700; Land O' Lakes, which has 1,340; and the Alto Dairy Cooperative, which has about 1,200 farmer producers.[6]

Smaller cheese factories will likely continue to close or consolidate.

Robert Wills of Cedar Grove cheese factory in Sauk County represents a growing number of young cheese makers who see a

future in smaller, more specialized cheese operations. Wills took over the Cedar Grove cheese factory in 1989. As he explained, "We've taken this plant from being primarily a commodity producer to primarily being a specialty producer, and that's been a huge process. Previously, ninety percent of our production was sixty-pound blocks of Colby. It all went to one customer. They made longhorns out of the blocks, packaged it, and sold it to Kraft, and they were rapidly putting us out of business. Some of these large packaging operations made their living putting small factories out of business." Some packaging firms maintained low prices and sometimes abruptly refused to purchase a factory's cheese.

Wills had to find new markets for Cedar Grove cheese. He found another buyer for about sixty percent of the Monterey Jack cheese, but as Wills pointed out, "When cheese prices took a dive in the early 1990s, they dumped us and left us with a warehouse full of cheese." Wills starting making cold calls to potential cheese markets, including Swiss Colony in Monroe, which Wills says saved Cedar Grove from going out of business. He now has a rule

5. "Foremost Farms changing the way it does business," *Wisconsin State Journal*, December 31, 1995.

6. Joel McNair, "Smaller Cheese Factories Holding Their Own," *Agri-View*, July 24, 1997.

that no single market will get more than fifteen percent of Cedar Grove's product. Wills now has increased his markets to some twenty major accounts.

Moving to specialty cheeses has worked well for many mid-size and smaller cheese factories, including Cedar Grove, which makes about forty different varieties of cheese, including specially flavored cheese curds and organic cheese. But educating customers is a major challenge. Wills constantly works at helping his customers know what makes a quality cheese product.

Randy Krahenbuhl, who operates the Prima Käse cheese factory in Monroe (a small factory making several specialty cheeses), says customer education is a major concern. "In the old days," Krahenbuhl said, "a customer would come into our cheese store and ask for a hunk of cheddar or Swiss and that was it. Some of these longtime customers have never heard of cheeses like Havarti or Asiago. They can't even pronounce the names."

National markets have changed and continue to change. Cheese factories, no matter what their size, must know what is going on in other parts of the country. In the early 1990s, Wills sold cheese to Texas and Denver markets, but now southwestern cheese makers can buy milk cheaper than Wills can, and he can't compete. "It's also possible for California cheese makers to ship their cheese to the East Coast and beat us on price, so we've decided to change and build our image as a high-quality manufacturer and search for markets that want that. We also emphasize our flexibility, that we can customize our products," Wills said.

In recent years, many Wisconsin cheese factories have had difficulty meeting Department of Natural Resources standards for wastewater disposal. Cedar Grove has recently received a grant to build a new type of biological treatment plant for its waste water. The system consists of a series of tanks in which natural materials interact with the waste. "In the last tank of the system, fish may be grown, the water is so pure," Wills says.

Management, record keeping, and keeping up with regulations are other challenges many smaller cheese factories face. Wills says he spends almost all of his time dealing with finance and regulations. Until recently, he didn't have enough sales to justify hiring bookkeeping and management staff. "This was a hurdle many smaller cheese factories faced, and they often decided to get out of the business," Wills said.

Colby and brick cheese are Wisconsin originals, developed by Wisconsin cheese makers. Colby was developed near the town of Colby; brick cheese was created in Dodge County.

Mrs. John Buhlman in the cheese and gift shop. Eau Galle Cheese Factory, Durand, 1996.

Many Wisconsin dairy farmers and cheese makers continue to believe that Wisconsin has many natural advantages for dairying. Few states have as ample a water supply, such good conditions for growing forage crops, and such generally good weather for dairy cows. With cheese plants located in many parts of the state, Wisconsin has considerable capacity for making cheese. Perhaps most important of all, Wisconsin has a long history of making quality cheese and a large number of highly qualified cheese makers.

7 How Cheese Is Made

Making cheese is at the same time remarkably simple and extremely complicated. It is both straightforward and mysterious. It is science and it is art.

The process begins with whole milk, the same milk we drink from a glass or pour over our cornflakes at breakfast. Add a little rennet, and the milk curdles. Soon you have a mixture of curds and whey. Drain off the whey, cut and press the curds into blocks, and you have cheese.

These are the fundamentals. The science and the art comes with the cheese maker, who with this basic method can turn out something as simple as cottage cheese and as complex as the finest, most delicate Camembert.

The Cedar Grove cheese factory, located near Plain in Sauk County, makes several kinds of cheese. Here is how cheddar cheese is made at their plant.

Three Cedar Grove tank trucks pick up milk from forty-five nearby farms. The trucks bring in about 100,000 pounds of milk each day, which by the next morning will have been converted into about 10,000 pounds of cheese.

Cheese making begins between 11 p.m. and midnight. It ends when employees finish wrapping and cleaning, about 9 p.m. the day after the process was begun. In those twenty-one or twenty-two hours, six or seven vats of cheese will have been made.

To start the process, milk is taken from storage tanks, filtered, and pasteurized by heating it to 161.5 degrees for fifteen seconds.

The cheese vat in the foreground is filling with milk.

—All the photos in this chapter were taken at the Cedar Grove cheese factory in 1997 by Steve Apps.

Mark Lins inoculates a vat of milk with a cheese culture. Different cheese cultures are used for making different kinds of cheese.

This kills common pathogenic bacteria (in other words, bad germs). The milk is then allowed to cool to ninety degrees, after which it is pumped into the cheese vats. Cedar Grove has three vats—one holds 22,000 pounds of milk; another, 14,000 pounds; and the smallest, 12,000 pounds.

A "starter" culture, a mix of bacteria and organisms, is added to the milk. It sours the milk by changing the lactose, or milk sugar, to lactic acid. Acid levels are watched carefully at various stages in the process, as different acid levels produce different varieties of cheese.

Dan Hetzel mops the sides of a cheese vat as it agitates in preparation for cooking.

To make yellow cheddar, a coloring agent called annatto is added to the milk. This is a tasteless, odorless, natural vegetable dye made from annatto seeds.

Rennet is then added. In earlier times, rennet was prepared from the fourth stomach of calves. Today, rennet is produced by bacteria that have been altered to produce the enzyme chymosin. This enzyme clots the milk. It is so powerful that it is mixed with milk in a ratio of 1:5,000.

Once the rennet has been added to the vat, the milk begins to coagulate. In about a half-hour, when the milk is the consistency

Mark Lins cuts thickened milk. The milk is thickened by the addition of rennet.

Dan Hetzel prepares to put paddles in a recently cut vat of cheese curds to begin agitating. In the background is cheese in hoops ready to be pressed.

With whey drained from the vat, Greg Laubmeier works Colby cheese curds.

of pudding, wire knives are pulled through the vat from one end to the other, both back and forth and across. The wire knives cut the coagulated milk into tiny cubes, which are called curds.

The curds are stirred gently. Steam is admitted into the outer lining of the vat, until the temperature of the curds is raised to 103 degrees. This "cooking" helps to separate the curds (the solid portion) from the whey (the watery liquid). The whey is then drained from the vat.

Once the desired moisture and acid levels are reached by heating, salt is added to the curds. Salt slows the starter. Without salt,

Dan Hetzel fills forty-pound cheese hoops with Colby cheese curd.

Greg Laubmeier prepares hoops filled with cheese curds for pressing. The pressing process knits the curds together into a solid block and removes whey.

the acid level would continue to build until the cheese crumbled.

The tiny curds are matted along the length of the vat and cut into eighteen-inch loaves. When the loaves are firm enough so that they can be handled without breaking, they are turned frequently. This step in the process is referred to as cheddaring. The loaves are then run through a cheddaring machine. This machine mills the loaves into small chunks of curd.

The curds are scooped into buckets and dumped into metal forms called "hoops." Hoops come in three parts with a cloth liner in the main part. Pins support the hoop's center section. When the

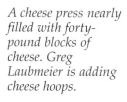

A cheese press nearly filled with forty-pound blocks of cheese. Greg Laubmeier is adding cheese hoops.

Melissa Chavez wraps Pepper Jack cheese into one-pound blocks.

pins are removed, the hoop collapses around the curd. The filled hoops are turned sideways and pressure is applied, compressing the curds into 42-pound blocks.

After pressing, individual curds lose their identity, and the pressed block has the familiar look of cheese. Finally, in a vacuum chamber, the blocks are placed in plastic bags, which are sealed. The cheese will now keep for years without forming mold. The sealed block of cheese is placed in a cardboard box, which has a wooden liner to protect the cheese and keep it square. It is then taken to the storage room and left to cure at about forty degrees.

Kathy Thering packs cheese for shipping.

The Cedar Grove cheese factory makes six main varieties of cheese: cheddar, Colby, Monterey Jack, muenster, farmers, and Butterkäse. Each of the varieties is different from the others in fat and moisture content, acidity, and texture. The driest and densest of the cheeses is cheddar. Cheddar cheese develops a sharp, fuller taste as it ages. Cedar Grove makes mild cheddar, which is aged up to a couple of months; medium cheddar, which is aged from four to six months; sharp cheddar, which is aged from six months to a year; and extra-sharp cheddar, which may be aged four years or more.

Adjusting the Process

Each type of cheese requires an adaptation of the cheese-making process. Cottage cheese is the least complicated cheese to make. Some people don't consider cottage cheese to be cheese because it is so different from cheddar. But cheese it is. The basic steps for making it are essentially the same as they are for other cheeses. First, you curdle the milk. (The milk, however, must be coagulated with a lactic acid starter instead of with rennet and enzymes.) Second, you separate the curds from the whey. The curd is not cut, pressed, or ripened, however, but is ready to eat almost immediately after it is formed.

Wisconsin produces about 300 different varieties, types, and styles of cheese.

Different cheeses will result depending on the starter culture used, how much the curds are heated, the amount of salting done, the way the cheese is pressed, and the number of times the cheese is turned while it is curing.

A page from the catalog of the Creamery Package Manufacturing Company, which made equipment for cheese factories.

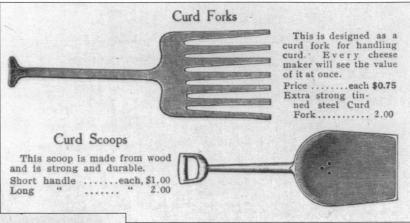

Curd Forks

This is designed as a curd fork for handling curd. Every cheese maker will see the value of it at once.

Price ....each **$0.75**
Extra strong tin-
ned steel Curd
Fork........... 2.00

Curd Scoops

This scoop is made from wood and is strong and durable.

Short handle ....each, $1.00
Long   "   .... "   2.00

The Acme Curd Rake

Cheese ripens from the inside out or from the outside in, depending on the variety of cheese. Cheddar cheese ripens from the inside out. No additional ripening agents are added while the cheese is maturing. The same holds for Swiss cheese. The bacteria responsible for creating Swiss cheese's special taste, and its holes, are added early in the cheese-making process.

Blue-veined cheeses are inoculated with a penicillium spore, which gives the cheese its bluish veins, unique taste, and characteristic aroma. Camembert, Brie, muenster, brick, and Limburger are surface-ripened, that is, ripened from the outside in. A bacterial broth or a mold is smeared on the outside of the cheese as it ages.

Over the years, the cheese-making process has become more scientific: laboratory-produced starters and rennet are now used, milk is tested for purity, and conditions are carefully controlled at the farm and in the factory. But despite these scientific advances, the basics of cheese making have changed little. Good cheese is still heavily dependent on the cheese maker, the maestro of the cheese factory.

8 *Cheese Makers*

Cheese makers are the soul of cheese making, for without them there would be no cheese. The cheese maker combines scientific knowledge with artful insight to produce a product that is healthy, tasty, and nutritious. A cheese maker starts work long before the sun rises and often continues after sunset or until the day's work is done. Many cheese makers see what they do as not just a job but a calling. There is something magical and mysterious about the way in which milk is transformed into cheese. The cheese maker oversees this process, day after day, always marveling at the wonder of it, and is constantly surprised by the challenges that emerge.

When the first cheese factories opened, men took over the task of cheese making from women who had been making cheese in farm kitchens. Some men were good at cheese making, others less so. But the market soon sorted out the good from the bad. People would not buy cheese of poor quality, at least not a second time. A few women became cheese makers in the factory system, most of them learning from their husbands or fathers. Edwin Fisher, a Sheboygan County historian, says that Katherine Feldmann, of the Town of Rhine in Sheboygan County, was the first woman factory cheese maker in Wisconsin. Mrs. Otto Wunsch was also a Sheboygan County cheese maker.[1]

---

1. Edwin Fisher, *The Cheese Factories of Sheboygan County* (Sheboygan, WI: Sheboygan County Historical Society, 1992), 9.

Life as a Cheese Maker

Cheese makers often worked and lived at several cheese factories during their careers. Conrad Frehner, who was born in 1870 and died in 1936, worked in twelve cheese factories in four Wisconsin counties and three Illinois counties. He began working

Katherine Feldmann, the first female cheese maker in Sheboygan County.

—From Sheboygan County Historical Research Center.

at the Juda Factory in Sylvester Township in Green County in 1895, not long after he was married. He then farmed for several years in Adams Township. He worked at the Dayton Factory next, in Exeter Township. Then he worked at three factories in Lafayette County: the Sanderson Factory, in Lamont Township; Lamont Central Factory, also in Lamont Township; and the Dublin Factory, in Darlington Township.

After that, Frehner worked at the Grand View Cheese Factory, in Seymour Township in Lafayette County; Linden Factory, in Linden Township in Iowa County; Pumpkin Center Factory, also in Linden Township; Bergen Factory, in Boone County, Illinois; Northwestern Factory, in Almena Township in Barron County; Zuercher Factory, in Ogle County, Illinois; and Scioto Mills Factory, in Stephenson County, Illinois.

Frehner's work record was compiled by his children forty years after his death. There is no indication as to why so many moves were made and whether it was his choice or not.

In contrast, Rodney Radloff was cheese maker at the Wild Rose Creamery Cooperative beginning in 1946. He stayed with the same cheese plant until it closed in 1987—forty-one years at the same place. He began as a hired man, earned his butter-making license, took the Dairy Short Course at the University of Wisconsin in 1949, and received his cheese maker's license. He became plant manager in 1964.

A present-day cheese maker, Jeff Wideman, worked several jobs before becoming cheese maker at the Maple Leaf Cheese Cooperative in Green County. Wideman was born and raised on a dairy farm; his family milked twenty-nine cows when he was

growing up. He began work at the Jefferson Center Cheese Factory in Green County in 1967, when he was seventeen. He worked there until 1977. In 1978, he worked as a supervisor for Universal Foods in Brodhead, where they made mozzarella cheese for pizza. After that, he became manager of a small privately owned plant near Jefferson, and there learned how to make many varieties of cheese. But the arrangement didn't work out, and Wideman left in 1980. At that time, he considered leaving cheese making and didn't work for several months. As he said, "I collected my thoughts, did a lot of fishing, and tried to decide what I wanted to do."

While he was out of work, several cheese factories contacted him, including the Maple Leaf Cooperative. At that time, they had only seven or eight farmers delivering milk. Wideman said he couldn't work there until they had more farmers; there just wasn't enough milk for the cheese makers to make a living. He talked to them in the early fall, and by the first of the next year they had increased their farmer numbers to eleven or twelve. He went to work for them on January 1, 1981.

Wideman has been with Maple Leaf since then, and has developed an outstanding reputation. He has won two consecutive United States cheese championships with his Monterey Jack wheels, and two Governor Sweepstakes awards for Gouda and Pesto Monterey Jack.[2]

Farmers bringing their milk to the Pumpkin "Punkin" Center Factory, north of Linden in Iowa County.

—From Jacob Frehner.

---

2. From a 1995 videotaped interview, on file with the Historic Cheesemaking Center, Monroe, WI.

Carlos Schroeder, now retired, was long associated with the Linden Cheese factory in Iowa County, which is now operated by his sons, Lloyd and David. Schroeder grew up in Potosi, the home of the famous Potosi Brewing Company, for which his father worked. The family lived a short distance from a cheese factory; Schroeder began working there the summer he was thirteen. This was during the Depression, and children were expected to find any job they could to help their families make it through. He gave his mother his paycheck, which was $25 each month.

In 1944, Schroeder's father quit the brewery, and the family moved to Monroe. Young Carlos then worked as a receiving clerk. Next the family moved to Hollandale to run a restaurant. Carlos started working for a cheese factory between Hollandale and Blanchardville. These were war years and labor was tight. At the age of sixteen, he was asked to run the business. Schroeder recalled that eight or ten farmers delivered milk to the factory.

Number of milk cows in Wisconsin:

1950-2.16 million
1970-1.8 million
1980-1.8 million
1990-1.7 million
1995-1.5 million

He married his wife Jeann in 1946 and bought the Pen Hollow Cheese Factory near Lone Rock in 1947. He operated this plant until he sold it in 1963, vowing to stay out of the cheese-making business. He and Jeann moved to Spring Green. But they had a growing family—nine children—and bought a little cheese factory near Bloomfield. By that time, some of the children were big enough to help out. They swept floors and turned, cut, and wrapped cheese. Schroeder recalled how his children played in one empty cheese vat while he and his wife made cheese in the other. The family continued to operate this cheese plant until 1973, when they bought the Linden plant.

Schroeder recalled good and bad times. A Dodgeville bank failed and he lost his savings. Another time, a major cheese sale fell through. He remembers making cheese around the clock during the 1970s.

Adolph Bach came to the United States from Switzerland with his family in 1923. In 1925, five-year-old Bach lived with his family on a farm. One day, a young couple in a new Dodge coupe came to visit. Years later, Bach said, "I thought a car like that was an unattainable object for our poor family."

Bach's father told him, "Cheese makers make good money, but it is very hard work." Bach continued thinking about cheese making as he did his farm chores. In 1937, the Bach family lost their farm in the Depression. Bach said, "I decided to become a

Unidentified cheese factory, Waupaca County, c. 1920.

—*From Wisconsin Cheese Makers Association.*

rich cheese maker and got a job for three months at $30 per month, seven days a week. But there was no dust or manure, and I loved it."

In 1938, a cheese maker in Darlington hired Bach at $60 per month for nine months. They made Swiss cheese wheels. He said, "I got two afternoons off all year, darn near slave labor as I look back at it now." In 1939, a cheese-making job opened at a factory near Mt. Vernon. Bach began working there, making Swiss cheese with a boss who was a native of Germany.

"In 1940," Bach said, "I got into big-time cheese making in the city—Madison. The plant had sixteen kettles. I made 120 dollars per month, which worked out to thirty-three cents an hour. By counting my pennies I put a hundred dollars a month into Postal Saving, when my salary increased to $130."

In 1940, Bach enrolled in the University of Wisconsin's Dairy Short Course. In the fall of 1941, he got his cheese maker's license and began operating his own cheese factory—Jones Valley, south of Barneveld. For salary he received thirteen percent of the cheese and cream sold. On the day before Pearl Harbor, December 6, 1941, he married, and borrowed $3,000 from his father-in-law and $750 from the Bank of Barneveld. He bought five kettles, a boiler, cream separator, and other equipment necessary for cheese making. His factory had a capacity of five wheels of Swiss cheese per day. In the early days, farmers brought their milk to his factory in ten-gallon cans. Some had trucks, some used teams and wagons, and one farmer had a new Ford 8N tractor with a three-point hitch and box on the drawbar that held his milk cans.

Bach said, "My cheese was always a bit above average quality because I insisted on good, well-cooled milk."

Floyd Burt received his cheese maker's license in 1935 and worked for his uncle, Lee Lepley, a cheese maker who owned the Liberty Pole Cheese Factory in Vernon County. Before that, he taught in the Retreat and Webber one-room country schools. In 1939, Floyd Burt and his brother, Durward, opened a cheese factory to serve the Bud area farmers. They worked together for six years before Durward moved to La Farge, where he owned and operated another cheese factory. Floyd stayed on to operate the Bud Cheese Factory for forty-six years. He sold the factory in 1985 to AMPI, which closed the plant.

The State of Wisconsin

EXECUTIVE OFFICE
MADISON
53702

WARREN P. KNOWLES
GOVERNOR

August 20, 1969

Mr. Floyd Burt
Viroqua
Wisconsin

Dear Mr. Burt:

Let me take this opportunity to extend my personal congratulations for your prize-winning entry in the cheese competition for the Sweepstakes Awards. Your quality production is one good reason Wisconsin has earned and maintained its position as America's Dairyland -- the best in the nation.

Your efforts have been an important part of the expansion of Wisconsin's dairy industry into a billion dollar business. Wisconsin's approximately two million dairy cattle on 65,000 farms produce about 18 billion pounds of milk each year. This means $850 million to dairy farmers with important additional benefits to processors, distributors, and all citizens in the community who benefit from this prosperity.

Without its outstanding dairy industry, Wisconsin would be hard pressed to provide the economic opportunities which now exist for its citizens. And without your efforts, Wisconsin's dairy industry would be itself hard pressed to maintain its competitive edge which makes the Wisconsin dairy industry so outstanding.

I am sure that I speak for all the citizens of our state when I offer you my heartiest congratulations on a job well done. Keep up the good work.

Sincerely,

Warren P. Knowles
Governor

WPK:rpc

Floyd Burt, Bud Cheese Factory, Vernon County, with the Governor's Sweepstakes Award for cheese making, 1969.

—From Floyd Burt.

A 1969 letter from Governor Warren Knowles to Floyd Burt congratulating him on his prizewinning cheese.

The interior of the Bud Cheese Factory, Vernon County, 1940. Floyd Burt, cheese maker, is on the far right.

—From Floyd Burt.

Burt recalled that in the early days, farmers hauled their milk to the cheese factory in buggies and wagons pulled by horses. Some farmers even used their new Model T Ford cars to haul milk. Burt saw many changes in the cheese-making industry. One of the most important was steady improvement in the quality of milk, and thus cheese of higher quality.

Burt's cheese was recognized for its quality many times. He only made cheddar cheese at his factory, and it won many ribbons, plaques, and other awards. Four times—in 1969, 1971, 1973, and 1974—he won the governor's cup for the top cheddar cheese at the Wisconsin State Fair. *Esquire* magazine recognized Burt's two-and-a-half-year-old cheddar as the best in the United States.

Albert Deppeler, a longtime Green County cheese maker, is considered by many to be the dean of cheese making—especially when it comes to Limburger and Baby Swiss. He managed the Chalet Cheese Cooperative from 1946 to 1992; Limburger was the main cheese made there for many years. Deppeler recalled the many challenges he faced:

"All our lives, we were at the mercy of the price the cheese dealers were offering. They would offer a price, I'd call another dealer, but they were all the same. It was as if you were owned by that dealer. Another dealer wouldn't even talk to you if the dealer in Monroe was buying from you," Deppeler said.

Deppeler recalled an interesting incident in 1970. "We had

Albert Deppeler of Green County, a longtime Limburger and Baby Swiss cheese maker, pictured next to the Limburger exhibit at the Historic Cheesemaking Center in Monroe, 1996. Deppeler also is an accomplished wood artisan.

more milk than I could use for Limburger and brick cheese. I could make it and sell it, but it wasn't at a profit."

At that time, Deppeler knew a university professor from Iowa who had been bringing his students to the cheese factory each year to show them how to make Limburger cheese. The professor, who was approaching eighty, took Deppeler aside. "This will be the last year I'll be bringing my class here," he said. "But I've got something for you."

The old professor gave Deppeler a book describing how to make Iowa-style Baby Swiss cheese. The professor said, "The citizens of Iowa paid good tax money for my research on this cheese, and not one cheese maker in Iowa has ever tried to make it."

The old professor then said to Deppeler, "Take the formula in my book, and you'll make good Baby Swiss the first day. But whatever you do, don't give away the formula. Make a little profit."

Deppeler took the old professor's advice. "We made, I think, about seven 14,000-pound vats of Baby Swiss cheese a day with that recipe."

Early Years

Before 1900, many Wisconsin cheese factories did not operate year-round. Dairy farmers, many of them recent converts from wheat growing, did not know how to care for their cows so they would milk throughout the winter months. Some farmers looked forward to winter when they could relax and avoid milking cows twice a day. Starting in December and continuing to April, the cheese factories closed. The cheese makers, their families and their hired men were out of work. Some cheese makers grabbed their axes and crosscut saws, and headed to the North Woods, where they worked in the logging camps during the winter months. It was a way for them to earn enough money to support their families until the snow melted in spring, the cows were turned out to pasture, and the farmers began milking again.

In Green County, some cheese makers who were single moved into the hotels for the winter months and picked up odd jobs. They enjoyed partying, and many stories circulated about their antics. As a game, some of these young men stood empty beer bottles at the end of the hall and rolled empty chamber pots at them to see how many they could knock down.

Wisconsin Cheese Makers Association

In the late 1800s, some unscrupulous Wisconsin cheese makers produced and sold filled cheese in which the milk fat was replaced with lard and other inferior fats. This activity badly tarnished the reputations of all Wisconsin cheese makers and the dairy industry in general.

Honest cheese makers—the vast majority—decided they needed to ensure high-quality products were being produced and that they were marketed well. They wanted their own organization to help them do this. Many were already members of the Wisconsin Dairymen's Association, but they believed the special problems cheese makers faced required a separate association.

Veteran cheese makers honored at Cheese Days in Monroe, 1935.

—From Jacob Frehner.

York Center Cheese Factory (Conrad Blanc and family, cheese makers), east of Blanchardville in Green County, 1912.

—From Historic Cheesemaking Center.

In 1893, they organized the Wisconsin Cheese Makers Association, which was formally incorporated in 1899. They encouraged members who met the following criteria to join: "Any person who is a practical cheese maker, and such other persons as are directly or indirectly interested in the manufacture and sale of unadulterated cheese may become members of the corporation by paying one dollar annually in advance and signing the roll of membership."

The Cheese Makers Association policed their own to ensure a quality cheese product. But more work was necessary in order to help the farmer patrons deliver higher-quality milk. The cheese makers took on this educational task, as difficult as it was. No cheese maker wanted to offend a farmer patron, because the cheese maker depended on the farmers' milk for their operations. Yet, a few farmers whose milk did not meet cleanliness and quality standards made it difficult for the cheese maker to produce good cheese.

In 1907, E. L. Aderhold of Neenah, in his president's address at the fifteenth annual meeting of the Cheese Makers Association, said, "It is the opinion of your president that during the life of this association the average skill of our cheese makers has increased very materially and that improvement in our milk supply with reference to its purity has been much too slow." He went on to chastise his fellow cheese makers.

The difference in the cleanliness of milk offered at different factories is astonishing, and I have found the widest range of difference existing in milk delivered to neighboring factories, in some cases located only a mile apart. That would indicate that the reason for accepting unclean milk cannot be ascribed to competition but rather to mismanagement. I have seen, at one factory, the manager reject over one-third of the milk offered, which was very dirty. He didn't reject it because it was dirty, but because the inspector was watching him. If dirty milk hadn't been acceptable to him, the farmers wouldn't have offered it in that condition. At another factory over half the patrons offered dirty milk and took it back home on the morning of the inspection. No one will think the majority of the patrons *happened* to have dirty milk on the same day. Their milk was dirty because of gross negligence. The manager had made a practice of accepting such milk and by so doing had placed his stamp of approval on the practice of such negligence."[3]

As the cheese-making industry grew, the state of Wisconsin stepped in to assist and to regulate the duties of cheese makers. For instance, the report of the Dairy and Food Commissioner of Wisconsin for 1895-1896 included these "Duties of Cheese Makers":

1. He shall be responsible for and make good in money, any loss that may be sustained from the making of inferior cheese through carelessness, neglect, or incapacity.

2. He shall keep a correct record of the weight of milk furnished by each patron and deliver the same to the secretary of the Company (or Association). It shall be the duty of the cheese maker to use his best endeavors to manufacture an article of uniformly fine merchantable cheese.

3. He shall test the milk of each patron from time to time, to assure himself that it is pure, wholesome, honest, and of good average quality.

4. He shall inspect the milk cans and report upon their condition to the Directors.

Stephen Moulton Babcock developed the Babcock Milk Test in 1890. The test measured the fat content of milk and provided a standardized way of paying farmers for their milk.

---

3. Wisconsin Cheese Makers Association, *Fifteenth Annual Meeting* (Milwaukee, WI 1907), 5-6.

5. He shall inspect the milk wagons and report upon their condition as to cleanliness, etc., to the Directors.

6. He shall enter in a pass book for each patron a record of the weight of milk received in his or her name.

8. He shall keep the factory and its utensils clean.

9. He shall care for the cheese until it is cured, or until one month after the close of the manufacturing season.

10. He shall see that the whey tank is thoroughly cleaned at least once a week.

11. He shall see that the surroundings of the premises are kept free from bad odors.

12. He shall use his best endeavors to advance the interest of the manufacturer and the patrons.

In case of the patrons or Directors shall find the weighing can, milk conductor, milk vats, curd sinks, curd cutter, cheese presses, or any other utensil, or the floor of the factory, in a filthy state, whereby the quality of the milk or cheese is liable to be injured, the sum of $1.00 for every such offense and every such utensil shall be deducted from the monies coming to the cheese maker from the manufacturer.

Several concerns were expressed in these rules. The cheese maker must pay close attention to sanitary and quality standards in and around his cheese factory. If he is negligent, then money will be deducted from his income. And he must follow good business practices—keeping track of patron's milk weights and recording them.

The Wisconsin Cheese Makers Association had great respect for farmers, even though they often were frustrated by their slowness to produce milk of the quality desired. At the thirteenth annual meeting of the association held in 1905 in Milwaukee, M. McKinnon of Sheboygan Falls responded to the president's address with these words:

Mr. President, there are some still left with us who were not only pioneers in the cheese business, but they were pioneers in the true sense of the word. They came to this great Badger state at a time when that poet who longed for a lodge in some vast wilderness could have had his longings

abundantly satisfied; for stretching from Lake Michigan on the east to the Mississippi on the west, was one vast contiguity of shade that must needs be hewn down, cut up, piled, and burned away before the pioneers could determine the character of the soil upon which they had located. But those pioneers belonged to that class of people who were willing to labor and to wait. They built their little log cabins, endured the hardships and privations incident to pioneer life in the fullest sense of the word, and they have been the eyewitness of great results. They have seen the forests vanish, the humble log cabin transformed into a mansion, the little log stables into magnificent barns, and cows are now feeding upon a thousand hills, supplying milk to more than a thousand cheese factories. These are unmistakable evidences of our wealth and prosperity.

Walnut Grove Cheese Factory, at the junction of County A and White Oak Road near Stewart (now Postville), Green County.

—From Historic Cheesemaking Center.

Licensing Qualifications

Today, only cheese makers who have licenses from the state of Wisconsin may oversee the production of cheese in the state. The Wisconsin Department of Agriculture, Trade, and Consumer Protection develops rules and regulations for the licensing of cheese makers.

To obtain a cheese maker's license, an applicant may serve an apprenticeship with a licensed cheese maker and must pass a

Mutual Dairy Cheese Factory, Kewaunee County, c. 1958.

—Rendering by Paul Raisleger.

written examination of legal standards and requirements for cheese composition, sanitation, labeling, and related information. To receive a license, an applicant must understand the grading of milk and milk ingredients; composition control; preparation and use of starter; problems of acidity control; common cheese defects and methods of overcoming them; yeast, mold, and bacterial control methods; and the arithmetic problems of practical dairying.[4]

Many applicants for the cheese maker's license have attended the University of Wisconsin's Dairy Short Course to obtain the information they need to pass the examination and become licensed cheese makers.

Time for Fun

Cheese making is hard work, and the hours are long. Once cows began producing milk year-round, the cheese makers worked year-round, seven days a week, every day of the year. A speaker at the 1905 annual meeting of the Wisconsin Cheese Makers Association put it this way: " ...in this great Badger state there has been and is today, one class of labor that has not been requited or appreciated. I refer to those who toil over the cheese vat, those who in years gone by have been working fully up to their strength, seven days in the week, thirty or thirty-one days in each month, nine, ten, twelve, or thirteen months each year." Most

---

4. *Wisconsin Cheesecyclopedia* (Madison, WI: Wisconsin Milk Marketing Board, 1995), 8.

cheese makers today would probably agree with this speaker's comments, even believing that the cheese maker's year sometimes seemed to have thirteen months.

This same speaker reminded those attending the meeting of how important social activities could be. He said, "The old saying, 'all work and no play makes Jack a dull boy' undoubtedly holds true when applied to a cheese maker. Then come out to these annual meetings, combine business with pleasure. You are entitled to at least three holidays each year and now that we are holding our meetings in this great city of Milwaukee, this metropolis of the state, this ideal place above all others in which we cheese makers convene either for business or pleasure, it is well to come here at least once a year and take note of city life."[5]

Swiss cheese makers knew how to have fun. Marion Burkhardt grew up in a cheese factory. She remembered card parties with neighboring cheese makers, and *hasenpfeffer* (marinated wild rabbit) feeds. A factory in which the family lived had two packing rooms. One was large enough for dances. For many years, a cheese-maker's ball was held in Monroe on the first Saturday in December.

Some of the cheese makers could play instruments and were in constant demand for parties and dances. John Bussman, who grew up in a cheese factory in Wisconsin and is now an active cheese maker in Warren, Illinois, recalled that both his mother and father played instruments and became part of a popular orchestra in the Green County area.

Nate Roth, who also grew up in Swiss cheese country, recalled:

> Many a Sunday afternoon was spent singing and yodeling. My grandfather and his friends would meet at his or a friend's home, and after a good meal the fun would begin. A pitcher of wine to fill the water glasses appeared (it was never abused), and then the music. Grandpa played the violin, one man an accordion, another a clarinet, and sometimes a bull fiddle would join the group. One of my uncles played a mandolin, and on occasion a zither added to the festivities.
>
> There were the old country songs of Switzerland sung in *Schweizerdeutsch*. Most of the men were Bernese Swiss and

---

5. M. McKinnon, "Response," in *Transactions of the Wisconsin Cheese Makers Association* (Madison, WI, 1905), 5.

the highlight of the afternoon was when they joined their voices in a good yodel. After the singing, conversation would reflect where they came from in their fatherland and what they were now doing in America. These men all became good citizens and were proud of their new land.[6]

Wrestling was also part of the Swiss cheese makers' social activities and was usually conducted on Saturday afternoons. Bussman recalled how the wrestlers would go at it in a field; Swiss wrestling it was called. Along with wrestling went weight lifting, and some wonderful tales about the strongest cheese makers in the area.

Emmentaler is the Swiss word for Swiss cheese.

In 1894, a famous weight-lifting contest took place at the Farmers Grove Cheese Factory in Green County. A report of it was signed by thirteen people who said they were eyewitnesses, attesting "…that the foregone is the truth and nothing but the truth." The contest was between Serey Rhyner, who was six feet three inches tall and weighed 245 pounds, and Ed Wenger, who was five feet eleven and three-quarter inches tall and weighed 208 pounds. Rhyner was a cheese salesman, and Wenger was a cheese buyer.

The contest was to see which man could lift a cheese vat containing about a ton of milk. Rhyner, who at the time was considered the strongest man in the Township of New Glarus, grabbed hold of the vat but couldn't budge it. Red-faced and somewhat embarrassed, he stood back to watch what Wenger could do.

Wenger suggested that John Burkhard and Alfred Arn crawl on top of the vat to add more weight. Wenger then proceeded to lift the vat of milk and the two men without difficulty, or so the story goes. As the signed proclamation states, "This is the heaviest weight any one man ever lifted in the history known to the human race."

Upon reading the proclamation, one could only conclude that everyone involved had been hitting the wine barrel a little too hard, especially those who signed as witnesses to the truthfulness of the event.

Cheese Makers and Wine

Swiss cheese makers enjoyed their wine. If you had stopped by an early Swiss cheese factory, chances are you'd be offered a glass of wine, a hunk of either Swiss or Limburger cheese, and a thick

---

6. Nate Roth, *An Old Cheese Maker's Life* (Monroe, WI: Historic Cheesemaking Center), 2.

slice of bread. John Bussman said, "My pa used to make four or five fifty-gallon barrels of wine. I'd have to pick the grapes which grew along the roadside fences."

The state inspectors who visited periodically did not want to see wine barrels sitting in the cheese factory. So some of the cheese makers built special cellars just for their wine. As Bussman said, "It was that important."

Bussman told about the time when several young men in the community decided they'd "borrow" some wine that they knew was stored in neighborhood cheese factories. These young wine drinkers built a cradle out of two-by-six lumber with the intention that they could roll a barrel of wine onto the cradle and carry it off. They had their eye on a cheese factory near Darlington, where they knew there were several barrels of good grape wine. They even sent out a spy to figure the lay of the land, learn where the wine was stored, and construct a strategy for stealing it.

The spy was a Norwegian fellow, in amongst a group of young Swiss men. He stopped at the factory, bought a little cheese, and inquired about a glass of wine.

"Sure, I've got wine," the cheese maker said. "Come with me."

The cheese maker led the young Norwegian down a miserable set of stairs to the cellar where the wine was stored. As he followed along, the Norwegian mentally noted what would be required to lug a heavy fifty-gallon barrel of wine up the steep, narrow steps.

Soon they arrived at the back of the dark cellar where the wine barrels rested.

"Been having some problems with our wine around here," the cheese maker said.

"What kind of problems?" the young Norwegian inquired.

"Wine stealing. Whole barrels are disappearing. Can you imagine that? These thieves lug off whole barrels of wine. I don't know how they do it."

The young Norwegian tried to keep a concerned look on his face as he listened to the cheese maker's story.

"But I think I've got the answer. Nobody's gonna steal my wine."

"How're you gonna prevent it?"

"See that shotgun over there?" It was fastened to the ceiling of the cellar and had a string attached to the trigger leading toward the door.

"Ya, I see it."

"Well, I hook that shotgun up so if somebody opens that door at night it goes off. Ought to kill the thief right in his tracks."

It is probably a good thing that the cellar was dark, so that the cheese maker could not see the color draining from the young Norwegian's face.

That was the end of wine stealing in that community.

Cheese Makers and Farmers

Some cheese makers couldn't get along with their farmer patrons, but they surely couldn't get along without them—no farmer patrons, no milk. No milk, no cheese.

Farmers often assumed that cheese makers were getting rich from making and selling cheese. Experienced cheese makers gave this advice to cheese makers new to a community: Don't buy an expensive car. Don't make it look like you're making any money. Farmers think you're rich. At least make it look like you're poor, even though you may be doing quite well.

Farmers and cheese makers often disagreed about the milk test. As each batch of milk was received at the cheese plant, it was tested for butterfat content. The higher the butterfat content, the more money the farmer received. But some farmers believed that the cheese maker was deliberately giving them a low test.

Many high schools in the state began offering courses in agriculture by the 1920s. High school agriculture students learned how to use the Babcock Milk Test and to test milk from their home herds. Cheese maker John Bussman recalled the time when a woman called him and said her son's milk tests were higher than those at the cheese factory.

"I explained to her that cows can vary from day to day," Bussman said. "I drove out to see her. She still couldn't understand why the cheese factory tests and her son's agriculture class tests were different."

"You either change your test at the cheese factory or we're going to switch cheese factories," the woman said.

"I'll double-check our cheese factory tests," Bussman said. "Sometimes we do have mix-ups."

But this didn't satisfy the woman. She switched cheese factories.

9 *Cheese Factories: Inside and Out*

Cheese factories come in all sizes and shapes. Some of the early ones looked like farmhouses; others resembled small warehouses. A few were built to look like stores, with false fronts extending above the roof line. A common cheese factory style in many parts of Wisconsin was a long, rectangular building, two stories tall with living quarters on the second floor.

Cheese factories were often of wood frame construction with barn boards placed vertically on the side walls, but it is not difficult to find cheese factories constructed of brick, glazed tile, or quarried rock. Edwin Fisher, in his review of Sheboygan County cheese factories, said that many of the early factories in that county were supported with hand-hewn beams, as were many Sheboygan County barns. The interior walls of many of these cheese factories were of lath and plaster construction. Some factories had a double layer of lath and plaster in some of the rooms to provide insulation.[1]

Where to Build a Cheese Factory

Where to build a cheese factory was an important question. Before the first board was nailed, those building a new cheese factory first checked to see if there were enough cows in the area to support it. In 1915, a University of Wisconsin bulletin had this

---

1. Edwin L. Fisher, *The Cheese Factories of Sheboygan County* (Sheboygan, WI: Sheboygan County Historical Society, 1992), 8.

Wild Rose Creamery Cooperative, Wild Rose, operated for many years as a creamery. The cooperative began making cheese in 1946, but also continued making butter. At one time the cooperative had 225 farmer patrons. It closed in 1987.

—From Rodney Radloff.

advice: "The first thing to do is to make a canvass of the surrounding country and find out how many cows can be depended upon to furnish either milk or cream to the factory. The best way to accomplish this is to circulate a paper, to be signed by each farmer, promising to send to the factory milk of uniformly good quality from a certain number of cows for a given number of years. To insure success there should be at least 400 cows for a creamery or 200 cows for a cheese factory with a good prospect of increasing this number in the near future."[2]

The physical placement of the building was also extremely important. Some old cheese makers recommended constructing a cheese factory against the side of a hill so that the back portion of the building was cool and thus would be a good place for curing cheese. For practical reasons, building the cheese factory near the neighborhood school made sense. Farmers could drop their children at the school when they delivered milk to the cheese factory each morning. When possible, a cheese factory was built on the side of the road, protected from blowing dust, and in a grove of trees, which cast shade during the hot summer months.

---

2. E. H. Farrington and G. H. Benkendorf, *Organization and Construction of Creameries and Cheese Factories* (Madison, WI: University of Wisconsin Agricultural Experiment Station, 1915), 5.

A good water supply was extremely important. It could come from a spring or a deep well that provided water at a temperature between forty-eight and fifty degrees.

Disposal of waste water was a serious matter. "If a factory site is so located that the drainage can be connected with a city or town sewerage system it is to be preferred to almost any other location," advised the university. "The next best place is one from which the factory drainage may empty into a river or creek that is so large as not to be polluted by such waste."[3]

A common complaint about cheese factories was the bad smell from spoiled whey. Pouring whey into a nearby stream or river solved the problem. But being too close to a river had its problems, too. Glenn Lepley worked two summers in the early 1950s for a cheese factory in Viola that was located about a hundred yards from the Kickapoo River. He recalled what happened after a heavy rain in July 1951.

Little Miss Muffet sat on her tuffet, eating her curds and whey. No doubt someone nearby was making cheese. Curds are the foundation of cheese. Whey is a by-product of the process.

> We had about eight inches of rain in six hours. I'd gone to work at three o'clock—that's a.m.—and my folks had given me the car to drive down to the cheese factory. I parked it out front of the factory on Main Street in Viola. About five-thirty or six, my mother called and wondered where the car was. I told her it was out front. She said, "You'd better check."
>
> I walked outside into knee-deep water and got over to my car, which was maybe thirty feet from the front door of the cheese factory. I opened the front door of the car, and the water sloshed in on the floorboards. I drove it up Main Street to higher ground, plowing water all the way. The Kickapoo was coming up. I went back of the factory to see what was going on, and all the milk cans we'd stored out back were starting to float off. I could see some dead animals floating in the river. One of our major problems was water pouring into the boiler room. It became necessary to shut down the boiler. We had to chain down the propane tanks that provided gas for the boiler so they wouldn't float away. We were making cheese in the vats at the time. The water ran in the front door and out the back, and it was up

---

3. Ibid., 21-22.

around the bottoms of those huge cheese vats. The cheese maker managed to salvage the cheese. There was water in the cheese factory most of the day. We had to rescue the cheese maker's wife who lived next door and got her out of there. You couldn't walk across Main Street in Viola that day. The water was too deep and the current was too strong. Don't know whatever happened to our milk cans. They probably ended up in Wauzeka.

Inside Arrangements

Early cheese factories had several rooms, with specific purposes. Milk usually was received in the intake room. In some older factories, the milk was received directly into the factory. Often, a four-foot-high platform was built in the intake room where the cans were emptied and the milk was weighed and tested. The milk then moved by gravity through a pipe to the cheese vats in the largest room of the building. There usually was also a boiler room, with an adjacent coal bin, and a cold storage room in which the cheese was aged.

The university recommended that the chimney be made of brick and be high enough to furnish a good draft at all times. For a fair-sized factory, the chimney should be about forty feet high and the flue twenty inches square. It should be lined with fire brick to the top.[4] Most of the time this advice was not followed,

Peck Dairy and Produce Company (A. W. Seefeldt, cheese maker), Deerbrook, c. 1920.

—From Wisconsin Cheese Makers Association.

4. Ibid.

and the cheese factory used an iron smokestack that stuck high above the roof. One way to identify a cheese factory in an old photo is to look for the smokestack.

Cheese-making Equipment

In his book, *Early Cheese Making in Wisconsin*, historian Norman Peters noted that the earliest cheese factories in Wisconsin needed the following equipment for making cheddar-type cheese:

* Two 5,000-pound cheese vats. They were constructed of wood and lined with tin.
* Fifteen cheese hoops (molds) of galvanized metal, about fifteen inches in diameter, each for a seventy-pound cheese. The hoop was lined with a bandage made of cotton cloth.
* One sixteen-foot horizontal wood press frame, with trough for whey drippings and a threaded screw attachment at the end. This would press a row of cheese hoops.
* Milk weigh can and scale, tinned steel curd knives, wood rakes, stirrers, scoops, buckets, and milk testing and weighing accessories.[5]

Early Swiss cheese factories used copper kettles rather than vats for making the traditional Swiss cheese wheels. The smallest factories had only one or two kettles; larger factories had several. Keeping the copper kettles clean was a constant challenge. When the day's cheese making was finished, factory workers scrubbed the kettles from top to bottom. As a worker at the Prima Käse cheese factory in Green County said, "If you don't clean a kettle well, it'll turn green. Then it takes twice the time to clean it."

In an old-fashioned Swiss cheese factory, all of the milk in one kettle made one wheel of cheese. A kettle might have held 2,000 pounds of milk; a wheel of cheese weighing 180 to well over 200 pounds resulted.

One important step in making Swiss cheese was slipping a piece of cloth under the curd so that it could be removed from the kettle. In order to put the cloth in place, the cheese maker had to lean well over the lip of the kettle. To avoid falling into the kettle, the cheese maker's wife or the hired man sometimes held the

Swiss cheese was made in 200-pound wheels because the Swiss government, during the Middle Ages, taxed cheese makers on the number of pieces of cheese they produced, not on the total weight. Forming the cheese into wheels became a tradition—one that continued after Swiss cheese makers came to this country.

---

5. Norman Peters, *Early Cheese Making in Wisconsin* (Fond du Lac, WI, 1989).

cheese maker's feet. At this point in the process, the curds and whey were still quite hot, perhaps 122 to 124 degrees.

John Bussman recalled the story of the new hired man who was asked to hold the feet of the cheese maker while he performed this delicate maneuver of leaning over the lip of the kettle. No one really knows what happened. Perhaps the hired man simply could no longer hold the cheese maker's feet. Maybe he slipped, or maybe he merely wanted to know what might happen if he let go. Well, he let go. The cheese maker tumbled into the hot curds and whey. He sputtered, spit, and swore when his head emerged from the hot mixture. He tried to fix his gaze on the man who had done the dastardly deed, but he was nowhere to be seen. The hired man had known the consequences of his action, and the moment he saw the cheese maker fall into the kettle he ran for the cheese factory door. The cheese maker caught a glimpse of him running down the dusty road, too far away to be pursued.

The next day, the hired man came back to reclaim his personal effects, for he knew he no longer had a job. He was wise enough to ask the sheriff to come along with him, just in case the cheese maker hadn't yet calmed down.

In recent years, Swiss cheese makers have begun using vats, retiring these old copper kettles.

Besides the cheese-making equipment mentioned above, early cheese factories had a boiler to provide power for the factory and steam for heating the cheese vats. Early boilers were wood fired; later ones used coal or propane gas. Hauling in wood for the boiler was a chore for the children who were too young to help with cheese making.

Cheese Factory Ownership

In the early years, cheese factories could be owned in at least three different ways. Proprietary factories were either owned by an individual or by a partnership of individuals. The cheese factory owners usually bought milk from farmer patrons and agreed to make butter or cheese for a definite price per pound. Any profits or losses were shared by the owners of the factory according to the amount of money each invested.

A second type of organization was a joint stock company. Joint stock companies were formed because some investors did not want the risk of a proprietary arrangement. In a joint stock company, stockholders could only lose the amount of money they invested. For instance, if a stockholder invested $1,000 he could lose no more than that amount, while in a proprietary arrangement he would be responsible for the debts of the company. With a joint stock company, all profits and losses were shared according to the amount of stock held by the individuals. Members of the company usually cast one vote for each share of stock held.

A cooperative was the third type of ownership. Farmer patrons were members of the cooperative and owned the factory. Each member of the cooperative had one vote no matter how many cows he milked or how much milk he delivered to the plant. The farmer patrons of the cooperative hired a cheese maker and his family to make cheese for them, usually on a percentage basis. According to Albert Deppeler, longtime Green County cheese maker, the percentage offered in 1910 was eight percent of gross income. In the 1920s, the percentage increased to nine percent, and by the 1940s it was up to ten percent in several cheese factories. In some Swiss cheese factories, as the amount of production increased, the percentage of gross income decreased.

Sometimes the cheese maker's salary was based on an amount of money per pound of cheese produced. The cheese maker was responsible for handling the farmer's milk, making it into cheese, keeping records, and selling the cheese. If it was necessary to employ a hired man (often the case) the salary for the hired man

Praag Cheese Factory (John J. Bai, cheese maker), Alma, c. 1920.

—From Wisconsin Cheese Makers Association.

came out of the cheese maker's salary; so did the cost of supplies to make cheese. In most cases, the cheese maker lived in quarters above or behind the cheese factory, which cut his living costs. If a hired man was employed, the cheese maker usually provided him with board and room at the cheese factory as well.

Wisconsin has been a leading state for agricultural cooperatives, especially those associated with the dairy industry. By 1940, most agricultural cooperatives in the United States were in Wisconsin, Iowa, and Minnesota. According to a 1940 United States Department of Agriculture publication, the oldest of the agricultural cooperatives were cooperative cheese factories, with these concentrated in Wisconsin and surrounding states. In that year there were 543 cooperative cheese-making plants in the Middle West, producing about one-fourth of all the cheese made in the country.[6]

The floor plan of Frigo Cheese Company in Lena.

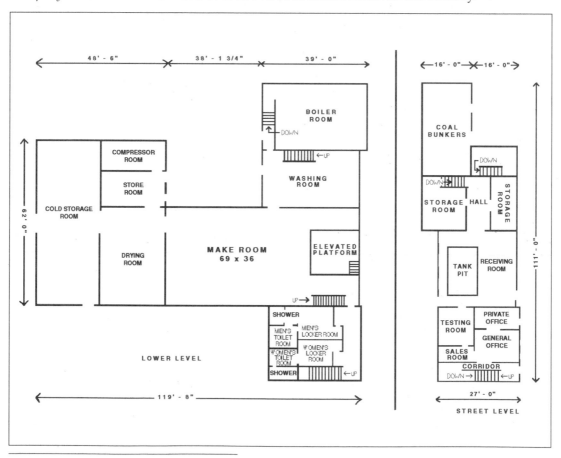

6. A. Stokdyk, "Cooperative Marketing by Farmers," in *Farmers in a Changing World: 1940 Yearbook of Agriculture* (Washington, D.C.: United States Department of Agriculture, 1940), 696.

Growing Up in a Cheese Factory

Albert Deppeler, who is still active in cheese making, was born in a cheese factory in 1923. "We lived above the cheese factory. The living quarters weren't insulated, and electricity didn't come through until 1937. We had our own well and had to pump water by hand."

Like many other little cheese factories of the day, the cheese factory in which Deppeler grew up, near Brodhead, was powered by a boiler that was fired with wood. "Some cheese factories owned wood lots," Deppeler said, "sometimes five or six miles away, where they got their firewood to heat their living quarters and to run the boilers at the cheese factory. Most farmers also had wood lots from five to fifteen acres that supplied firewood. Sometimes farmers would bring wood to the cheese factories—oak and elm mostly."

Deppeler remembered the old wood-fired boiler at the home cheese factory. "The boiler made steam, and had a small vertical steam engine. You had to have at least forty pounds of steam in the boiler to run the steam engine. If you had enough steam left over, you'd pump water for the next day. If there wasn't enough steam, I pumped water by hand when I got home from school."

In addition to pumping water, Deppeler had other jobs around the cheese factory. "I started helping out when I was four years old. At first I wrapped cheese. It was one-pound Limburger cheese packages. I'd lay the paper down, put the cheese on it, roll it, and seal both ends. By the time I was ten years old, I was still wrapping cheese, but now I was expected to do it twice as fast."

John Buhlman grew up in a cheese factory near Eau Galle, in northwestern Wisconsin. "When I was a kid, my job was to haul slab wood for the boiler. It wasn't much fun when it was thirty-four below zero. There wasn't any room to store it, and the wood pile was 500 feet from the door, so we had to use a wheelbarrow to haul it in. Got the slab wood from a nearby saw mill. I hauled ten to fifteen wheelbarrow loads every day. Big ones. Used the wood to power the plant, before electricity. We had a line shaft that distributed power throughout the factory."

The factory's boiler powered the line shaft. A line shaft is a metal axle with a series of pulleys fastened to it. Belts running from these pulleys powered various pieces of equipment in the cheese factory.

Cheddar cheese, the most popular cheese in the world, is named for the village of Cheddar in Somersetshire, England, where it was first made in the 1500s.

Jacob Frehner, Monroe, points to the location of the Green County Cheese Factory in which he grew up. The map can be found at the Historic Cheesemaking Center in Monroe.

Kids often got into trouble in their father's cheese factory. John Buhlman said, "I got thrown into one of those vats. I was about twelve or so. One of the hired men threw me in; they had just taken all the cheese out, so the whey was still in there, so he just picked me up and threw me in. I probably was picking on him, slapped a little whey on him. He just grabbed me and threw me in. I crawled out, smelling like whey."

Jacob Frehner from Green County grew up in a cheese factory and had the job of helping keep the boiler operating. "I was eight years old. My brother and I had to fill the boiler with water every day. Another of our jobs, besides hauling out the ashes and shoveling coal, was to pump water."

Nate Roth recalled the coal-fired boilers. "It took lots of heat to run a cheese factory…. The cheese maker would order a rail car load of coal, which was placed on the nearest siding. The patrons of the factory then brought trucks or wagons and shoveled all the coal by hand, first into a truck or wagon and then into the coal shed. On a hot day, this was hard work, and by night the hauler was as black as the coal."[7]

Cheese factory machinery was dangerous. Robert Kessler spent his boyhood years in a cheese factory. He became a cheese grader. When he was a youngster, he lost a finger in the belt of a steam-driven pump jack. Jeannette Faken Barta grew up in the

---

7. Roth, *An Old Cheese Maker's Life*, 2.

The original Forestville Cheese Factory in Door County. To the left is the cheese plant; the middle section was the cooler. In the early days, the cheese was cooled with ice blocks cut from the river. The ice was stored and covered with sawdust to keep it from melting. To cool the cheese, the sawdust was washed off and the ice was put in the cooler. Later, a refrigerator unit was installed. The section to the right was the sawmill.

—From Mrs. Donald Barta.

Forestville Cheese Factory in Door County. She said, "Our parents were very cautious about letting us in the factory when the machinery was running. The floors were always slippery because they were washed down so often. One time I was told to call Dad for dinner. As I ran, I slipped, and my hair caught in a belt that was running the cream separator. Luckily Dad was there to pull me out. The belt burn on my wrist is still visible today."

Cheese-factory life could be dangerous in other ways, too. Marion Burkhardt grew up in a Green County cheese factory and did not know how to speak English as a little girl. One day her father told her, "It is time for you to learn English."

He invited the neighbor girl to teach his daughter how to speak English. The lessons seemed to be going well. Marion enjoyed them, and the neighbor girl liked her role as teacher.

One day another neighbor came to visit, and Marion's father asked her to say something in English. He proudly stood by while she rattled off a string of English words. Unfortunately they were all cuss words. End of English lessons with the neighbor girl.[8]

Cheese Factory Life

Nate Roth recalled a typical day in a 1930s cheese factory.

A small country cheese factory was usually operated by a cheese maker, his wife, and the hired man. Early risers, they fired the boiler and prepared for the first milk delivered by the farmers. After the day's batch of cheese was made up

---

8. From a 1995 videotaped interview on file with the Historic Cheesemaking Center, Monroe, WI.

and the equipment was washed and steamed, they went up to the packing rooms where boxes were assembled in which brick and Limburger were shipped. Cheese was washed, Limburger 'smeared,' and in a Swiss factory, the wheels were washed and turned. After cooldown, the boiler needed cleaning. Some makers headed for the woods and 'made wood' and also kindling. Little bundles of branches were cut in short lengths and bundled in a 'schnitzel bank.' The dried bundles made excellent fire starters for the boiler."[9]

Winter was always a problem in a cheese factory. Rodney Radloff, longtime Wild Rose cheese maker, said, "I just hated winter coming. We always had freeze-ups. Only time we'd have problems with the boiler was in winter. I spent quite a few nights down there nursing the boiler along so we'd have enough steam to get started in the morning."

Frozen milk was another winter obstacle many cheese factories faced. Radloff recalled those times well. "Some days the milk would come to the factory frozen in the cans. We couldn't get it out. We had a thawer that circulated hot water; it would thaw the milk. But we still had to do a lot of pounding before we could dump the milk. It was something we had to put up with. A truck would break down and sit out on the road for an extra four or five hours. It would come in at nine o'clock at night and unload. It'd be twenty below zero and the whole load would be pretty well frozen."

Jeannette Barta recalled the Depression years. She remembered talk of a milk strike because milk prices were so low and farmers wanted to do something about it. "A group of farmers decided to dump their milk to cause a shortage and bring up the price. Not all the farmers agreed to this and there was talk of violence. Not only were the farmers who continued shipping their milk threatened, but the cheese makers were too. Of course, one of the cheese makers still making cheese was my dad. He tried to tell my mother not to worry because he had a loaded shotgun in the factory. Somehow this didn't console my mother very much," said Barta.

Cheese factory work was family work. Jeannette Barta recalled helping to make wooden cheese boxes in the factory that her father, Charles Faken, operated. She said:

---

9. Roth, *An Old Cheese Maker's Life*, 1.

Charles and Hilda Faken with their son, Roger. This is the first truck that Faken owned. He used it to haul logs from the Maplewood swamp for his sawmill, which was attached to the cheese factory. Faken not only made cheese, but he also made wooden boxes in which cheese was shipped. The truck is loaded with wooden cheese boxes with each box designed to hold two ten-pound blocks of cheese.

—From Mrs. Donald Barta.

In the early days Dad made daisies, cylindrical twenty-five-pound blocks of cheese, or midgets, which were twelve-and-a-quarter-pound cylinders. When he made these cheeses he bought the round veneer boxes from the Rio Creek Veneer Factory. One day, the cheese buyer asked Dad to make smaller cheeses. He switched to making ten-pound squares. They really weren't square but about five inches wide by fifteen inches long. Two of these blocks of cheese fit into a wooden box. Dad decided he could make the boxes himself. He owned a swamp in Maplewood, and with the help of another man he made logs out of poplar and basswood trees. He hauled them back to the cheese factory where he had a sawmill on the south end. Here he ripped the logs and squared them. He also had a cut-off saw, shingle saw, dovetailer, and planer. The four dovetailed sides were pounded together with a regular hammer, and if we kids wanted some extra money, we nailed together the four sides. We got a quarter for nailing together a hundred boxes.

The Faken children also helped out with the cheese-box covers, which were a single piece of veneer and had to be purchased. They arrived green and had to be piled so they dried properly. "What a backbreaking job it was," she recalled. "This job we were expected to do without pay. I can't tell you how many slivers I dug out of my hands."

Neighboring farm boys sometimes got in on cheese factory activities. Kim Tschudy remembers when he was eight or nine years old. "My uncle would take me along with him to the neighborhood cheese factory to deliver the milk. Several other of the young bucks hoping to become studs would stand around and drink whey, telling their younger charges, 'That's how you get hair on your chest.'"

"After I looked at the whey and smelled it, it didn't seem all that necessary to have hair on my chest," Tschudy said.

At one time, almost every cheese factory operated seven days a week, twelve or fourteen hours a day. Today, thanks to refrigerated storage facilities, cheese factories can store milk so they do not have to make cheese on Sundays. The schedules during the week can be gruesome, however. For instance, at the Krohn Dairy in Kewaunee County, the basic shifts are 6 a.m. to 3:30 p.m., and from 3:30 p.m. until the work is finished. In summer this may mean 1 a.m. In winter, when there is less milk, it is more likely 11 p.m.

"We have a person who comes in at 2 a.m. to start filling the cheese vats. Another worker joins him at 4 a.m. as they prepare for the main shift to come in at 6 a.m. It is a complicated work schedule, but a necessary one for today's large and highly mechanized cheese factory," says Jean Krohn Doell.

Floyd Burt, longtime owner of the Bud Cheese Factory in Vernon County, said, "I started working in a cheese factory with no electricity. It was back when we worked twelve or more hours a day, seven days a week. The farmers' milk had to be made into cheese the very same day as there was no way for farmers to cool it other than in a stock tank. It was up to the cheese maker to make a quality product or it would not sell."

Especially considering today's standards, the Bud Cheese Factory was small. It had four full-time employees plus one full-time milk hauler. The factory took in from 40,000 to 50,000 pounds of milk a day, which translates into 4,000 to 5,000 pounds of cheese per day.

A few of Wisconsin's smaller cheese factories continue to operate as family affairs. In a few instances, the cheese maker and his family still live above the cheese factory. But in most cases, the cheese maker lives away from the factory, and he may be but one of several cheese makers employed by the plant.

Blind cheese is Swiss cheese that lacks eyes.

10 *Cheese Buyers, Graders, and Inspectors*

In addition to farmers and cheese makers, several other people are important to the cheese industry.

Cheese Buyers

In the early years, some cheese makers sold their cheese directly to grocers. This arrangement often did not work well, however. Cheese is perishable, and it had to be moved fairly quickly from producer to buyer or it had to be stored in a cool place. Some cheese factory owners in a community pooled their resources and built cool-storage facilities. Remnants of such a storage place can be found built into a hill west of Monticello.

Many cheese makers turned to cheese buyers, who functioned as wholesalers, buying cheese from various factories and then selling it to grocers and other retail markets. Cheese buyers usually owned warehouses in which they stored, packaged, aged, and then distributed cheese to various markets. In the years when cheese factories closed during the winter months, the cheese buyers relied on stored cheese to provide an even supply to their customers. A pair of cheese warehouses, one of brick and one of quarried rock, still stand near Monticello's old train depot.

Cheese buyers are still important to the cheese industry. Pattie LaCombe is a cheese buyer for Schreiber Foods, Inc. in Green Bay. Her official title is purchasing manager, which means, in her words, "I [negotiate for and buy] cheese from cheese companies throughout the country and offer a short-term or long-term

Remnants of an early underground cheese storage facility in Green County, 1996. The warehouse, with a stone front, is built into the side of a hill. Often several area cheese factories built and shared storage places such as this one.

contract to them."

Schreiber Foods, Inc. is the largest private-label cheese company in the world. "What we do is package and prepare cheese for our customers, who are mostly in the food-service or retail area. Some of our customers include McDonald's, Hardees, and Burger King. We deal mostly with cheddar cheese and ship it to our customers in five-pound loaves or shredded in five-pound bags for customers like Taco Bell," said LaCombe.

When buying cheese, "I first make sure the cheese factory is a United States Department of Agriculture approved factory. I examine their methods of sanitation control, their food-safety program, and the volume of cheese they produce a year and whether it fluctuates a great extent. I also consider the type of cheese they are producing and whether they would be willing to work with us."

LaCombe tries to establish a relationship with the cheese factory to assure that the cheese is of the highest quality. "We have contracts that run from thirty days to six months with cheese factories. The contract specifies quantities of cheese they will make available."

Most of what she buys is cheddar cheese that is less than twenty days old. Currently she is buying from six to ten plants in Wisconsin, and from plants in California and Oklahoma. She is also a licensed cheese grader.

Doran Zwygart started buying cheese in 1940, went into the service during World War II, and then bought cheese between 1945 and 1988. He worked for the Armour Company for many years, and then formed a small company of his own in 1980. He is also a cheese grader, licensed for Swiss, cheddar, brick, and muenster.

He recalled some of his early days as a cheese buyer, when he bought cheese directly from the little cheese factories. "There was sort of a gentlemen's agreement. You bought cheese from a cheese factory for a certain period of time—you took whatever they manufactured. However, if they wanted to leave [to sell to another buyer] they seemed to think it was all right. But if the buyer dropped them, it was a terrible calamity, because they said they had no place to go. It was a kind of one-way street."

Zwygart contacted the cheese factories, graded the cheese, and then bought it. "You had to pay the money promptly—there was no delaying of payment. The farmers were waiting for their money," Zwygart said.

He recalled the time, in the 1950s, when he couldn't find enough brick cheese. Dodge County was a major producer of brick in those days, but it couldn't meet the demand. Zwygart would go to some of the cheddar cheese factories and encourage them to make brick cheese while he waited for the Dodge County production of brick to increase. The agreement was that the cheese maker would make a certain amount of brick and then go back to making cheddar.

One day, Zwygart phoned a particular cheese maker to tell him that he couldn't buy any more of his brick cheese, that he had enough.

"Will you come up?" the cheese maker asked. So Zwygart drove to the cheese factory.

When he got there, the cheese maker began pouring glasses of wine for Zwygart. After a while, Zwygart said, "I gotta go home."

The cheese maker asked, "Can I make any more brick cheese?"

"No, you can't," Zwygart replied. "I've got enough."

"Ah, shucks," the cheese maker said. "I thought if I gave you all that wine you'd say, 'Ya, sure.'"

National Cheese Exchange

The roots of the National Cheese Exchange go back to 1873, when cheese factory operators were looking for a method of selling cheese that was more fair to the cheese maker. Cheese boards, made up of buyers and sellers, were established, offering a competitive market for cheese makers. At one time, more than fifty such boards existed. Later, a type of auction sale emerged. A cheese maker would list his cheese on a black board and then call for bids. Both the offer and the bids were termed "calls," and these black boards became known as "call boards."

The cheese board that was established in Plymouth on May 22, 1879, evolved into the Wisconsin Cheese Exchange. (The exchange was officially organized on April 24, 1918; it moved to Green Bay in August 1956.) The Wisconsin Cheese Exchange adopted the call-board method of trading in 1900. Many problems existed with this approach, however. Sellers could not name a price for their cheese, bids offered were not firm and could be withdrawn at any time, and sellers were not required to deliver cheese in strict compliance with what they offered.

To have a good supply of high-quality cheese, cheese buyers once more established direct connections with cheese factories. However, buyers often contracted to buy all of a factory's output for a specified time, usually a year. This arrangement saved the cheese maker time and effort, but new problems emerged. Now the cheese dealer, especially during the summer months when cheese production was high, often had more cheese than he had markets. Cheese buyers began offering cheese for sale on a call board.

When the Wisconsin Cheese Exchange opened in 1918, dealers as well as cheese makers could become members. By 1921, however, cheese makers were selling little or no cheese on the exchange. It served mostly as a way for cheese buyers to sell their excess cheese. During World War II, new rules were passed that allowed the federal government to trade on the exchange. The federal government purchased more than 134 million pounds for the Armed Services and other government programs.

For many years, the National Cheese Exchange—the name was changed in June 1975—offered a trading session of thirty minutes each Friday in Green Bay. On average, about twenty members attended. The president rang a bell and trading began. Members offered the cheese they had to sell, or they bid for cheese they were interested in purchasing. The trading unit was a rail car load of cheese consisting of not less than 40,000 pounds or more than 43,000 pounds. Each offer and bid was posted on the board in the

The Wisconsin Cheese Makers Association was organized in 1893.

order that it was made. The offers and bids specified the price per pound, type, and number of carloads of the cheese to be sold or purchased. It was a cash market in which buyers paid sellers within seven days and shipment was made within three days following the trading session. The cheese offered was limited to forty-pound blocks and 500-pound barrels, primarily of cheddar cheese.

For several years, cheese prices on the National Cheese Exchange were used to help set farmers' milk prices. In the fall of 1996, Cheese Exchange prices dropped dramatically. Along with cheese prices, milk prices plummeted. Farmers were outraged. They took out much of their anger on the Cheese Exchange, accusing the long-standing cheese market of price manipulation.

Controversy swirled well into 1997. In March, it was announced that the historic exchange would cease operations. At 10:33 a.m. on April 25, 1997, Richard Gould, president, sounded the bell, ending trading in Green Bay not only for the week but forever. After forty-one years of cheese trading in Green Bay, the activity moved to the Chicago Mercantile Exchange. The first trading day in Chicago was May 1, 1997. The price of forty-pound blocks of cheese closed at $1.15 per pound, three cents below the price offered on the last day of trading in Green Bay.

The Cheese Exchange had served as an alternative source of supply and a place for firms to sell surplus cheese. Something less

Cheese warehouses near the old depot in Monticello, 1996. The one on the left is made of brick; the one on the right is constructed of fieldstone. Many tons of Green County cheese were stored and shipped from these warehouses.

*Hillside Cheese
Factory (Cl. Reisner,
cheese maker),
Bonduel, c. 1920.*

*—From Wisconsin
Cheese Makers
Association.*

than two percent of the cheese sold in the United States was sold through the National Cheese Exchange, but it was a valuable market alternative for its members. In recent years, membership ranged from thirty-five to forty-five. The majority of the members were cheese processors, dealers, brokers, and cooperatives, including Kraft Foods, Schreiber Foods, Mid-America Dairymen, Beatrice Foods, and Foremost Farms.

Cheese Graders

Wisconsin cheese graders, like cheese makers, must be licensed.[1] The state Department of Agriculture, Trade, and Consumer Protection administers the licensing program. To earn a license, applicants must pass a written examination that includes the laws and regulations pertaining to the type of cheese the applicant wishes to grade. Applicants are examined in the following areas: grading terminology, record-keeping requirements,

---

1. Information about cheese-grader requirements and cheese grades from *Wisconsin Cheesecyclopedia*, 7-13, and Doran Zwygart.

pasteurization temperatures and requirements, moisture and milk-fat requirements, cheese factory procedures for bulk cheese, starter control and effects of starter activities, knowledge of all possible grades of cheese, ability to calculate moisture and fat content from cheese samples, and knowledge of cheese styles and weight standards.

Each licensed cheese grader receives an identification number, and all cheese graded by that grader carries that number. As early as 1921, Wisconsin developed quality grades for the major varieties of cheese made in the state. It became the only state to mandate cheese grading.

To determine the appropriate grade for a given cheese, cheese graders look for flavor, body and texture, color, finish, and appearance. Grades used are: Wisconsin Certified Premium Grade AA, Wisconsin State Brand and Wisconsin Grade A, Wisconsin Junior, Wisconsin Grade B, Undergrade, and Not Graded. These grades are found on cheddar, Colby, Monterey Jack, brick, and muenster cheese. Swiss cheese has a separate grading system.

Grade AA represents the highest quality cheese. A cheese with this grade has met all the standards. The grade designation, along with the cheese grader's license number, appears inside of a

The old railroad depot in Monticello from which tons of Swiss and Limburger cheese were shipped, 1996.

miniature outline of the state. Grade A and Wisconsin State Brand, which are interchangeable, represent top-quality cheese. It is a designation awarded to the majority of cheese produced in Wisconsin. Wisconsin Junior requires the cheese to grade high on flavor, but there may be slight defects in body and texture, or finish and appearance. A small amount of cheese falls in this category. Wisconsin Grade B must have a fairly pleasing cheese flavor but typically has slight defects in body and texture or finish and appearance. Both Wisconsin Grade B and Wisconsin Junior are used mostly as an ingredient in processed foods and Process cheese. Undergrade does not meet the above grade requirements. And "Not Graded" means the cheese meets no specific grade standards.

Cheese age refers to the time that has passed from the date of manufacture. Cheese made from nonpasteurized milk must be aged a minimum of sixty days.

The age requirements for cheddar cheese are:

- Fresh or current: not more than four months old.
- Medium-cured: at least four months but not more than ten months old.
- Aged: more than ten months old.

Some cheese factories add additional age categories. For instance, the Cedar Grove cheese factory in Plain includes a "Sharp" category for cheese aged six months to a year, and "Extra Sharp" for cheese aged more than a year.

Wisconsin Swiss cheese receives a grade of either A, B, C, or D. Flavor is a major criterion that graders use, but a cheese may be downgraded for appearance. A major consideration is the size and consistency of eyes in the cheese. Swiss cheese graders also look at body, texture, color, and finish.

A trier is the device cheese graders use to remove a plug of cheese for grading.

Most of the Swiss cheese produced in Wisconsin is Grade A. Much of the rest is Grade B. To slip from Grade A to B, a cheese may have slight defects in body and texture, including eye formation, finish and appearance. Grade C Swiss has slight to definite defects in flavor, body, eye formation and texture, finish and appearance, and color. Grade C Swiss may have eyes that are too small or too large, or eyes may be missing (this is referred to as "blind" cheese). Grade D Swiss (some call this cheese "grinders")

Johnson Cheese Factory (Walter Tuescher, cheese maker, 1945-1969), on Highway 176 northwest of South Wayne, Lafayette County.

—From Historic Cheesemaking Center.

has defects that range from definite to pronounced; for instance it may be consistently blind. Most of Grade D cheese goes into processed foods.

Doran Zwygart remembered his days grading Swiss cheese, when there was often disagreement between the cheese maker and the grader about the quality of a wheel of Swiss.

"Swiss cheese was difficult to grade. The weight of a wheel of Swiss cheese could range from 130 pounds to 290 pounds, and the diameter could range from twenty-seven inches up to thirty-eight inches," Zwygart said. "And besides that, you could put in a cheese trier [a metal device for extracting a small core of cheese] and get four grades in one wheel. That's where the trouble came. If the cheese ran uniform it was easy to grade, but if it was uneven, it was very difficult. I liked to see two or three eyes on the cheese core." He used an eight-inch trier.

Zwygart explained that a grader first "tried" Swiss cheese about eight inches in from the rim. The salt in the rim prevented eyes from forming, and it was often too firm out there. He'd push the trier into each side of the wheel a couple of times, and every wheel was graded without exception.

The system for indicating the grades for Swiss cheese involved gouging a mark on the top of the wheel of cheese with a little knife. One mark on top was Grade A. Two marks forming a "T" was grade B. Grade C was three marks forming a capital "I." A grade of D was a cat-and-rat-type sign (#) formed with four marks.

Inspectors

State and federal inspectors regularly visit cheese factories. In this way, both quality and sanitary standards are maintained. However, sometimes cheese makers do not appreciate inspector visits. John Bussman remembered when a state inspector stopped by a Swiss cheese factory.

The inspector finished his look around and then said to the cheese maker, "Jake."

"Ya," replied the cheese maker.

"You got a crack in your floor here."

"Floor's clean, ain't it?" replied Jake.

"You still gotta put in a new floor."

"Listen you damn fool," said Jake. "I don't make cheese on the floor."

Jake put in a new floor.

In recent years, the Department of Natural Resources has become increasingly interested in what happens to wastes created by cheese factories, especially if the plant is located near a pond or stream.

The Wild Rose Creamery Cooperative was located on the banks of the Pine River. In the early days, it was common practice to dump waste water directly in the river. By the 1950s, the plant had developed a pumping system and a pipeline so the waste water could be sprayed on land a half-mile from the river. This worked well as long as the pump worked properly. One day the pump failed. And as luck would have it, a DNR official saw the waste water draining into the river from the overflow pipe. Cheese maker Rodney Radloff recalled the incident this way:

"It happened about noon. I was home for lunch. The DNR guy

was waiting when I got back. He had some Polaroid photos of the waste water running into the river and I had to go to court."

As soon as Radloff learned about the problem, he hooked up a spare pump, but he still had to go to county court.

"When I got to court, I explained the whole situation to the judge who listened carefully to what I had to say and what the DNR fellow had to say."

Finally, the judge looked up and said, "You seem to have done all you could possibly do. I'm not giving you a fine."

"The guy from the DNR didn't look too happy," Radloff said.

Ferdie Nachreiner, retired owner of the Cedar Grove cheese factory, had his problems with inspectors, too. He recalled the time when there had been some problems with milk tests—a common problem. Most farmers thought the test they received ought to be higher than that recorded by the cheese factory. (Milk tests are used to determine the price paid for milk.) The state sent five inspectors to the Cedar Grove factory.

"You understand," Nachreiner said, "the milk can would come in on a conveyer, you'd dump the milk, then you'd put the can in the can washer. My intake [for the cans] was about that high off the ground." Nachreiner measured about four feet with his hands as he talked. He described where the equipment was located. "Let's assume here is the can washer and here is the dumping tank, and the conveyer belt comes here—this was a short conveyer. Four guys stand over you, watching. The fifth guy is about to take the milk sample. I was standing here dumping the milk and putting the empty can in the can washer. This fellow bends over to take the sample—he had a rear end about this wide." Nachreiner held his hands about three feet apart.

"This fellow with the test jar, well, he leans down. Now here is the wall and right here is the vat—with about this much milk in it." Nachreiner's gesture suggested about three feet.

"Well, when the inspector went to lean over, by mistake I bumped him, and he fell into the vat. I pretended it was an accident. I was the first guy down there to fish him out. You had to see this to believe it. It was comical. The guy really, sincerely, thought it was an accident, he never carried a grudge. But he never came back to my factory either.

"I think what tickled me the most, here's five inspectors—and I'd say there was probably $2,500, $3,000 of milk in the vat he fell

Cheese ripens from the outside in or from the inside out, depending on the variety of cheese. Cheddar and Swiss ripen from the inside out. Brick, muenster, and Limburger ripen from the outside in.

*Scrubbing a Swiss
cheese kettle.
Prima Käse
cheese factory,
Monticello, 1997.*

—Photo by Steve Apps.

into. They never made us dump the milk. Maybe the inspector added a little extra flavor. I think that was the highlight of my forty-two years in the cheese-making business. Ordinarily, I had a good relationship with inspectors. I thought we had good ones, very humane, but that deal—if they'd found out, I'd probably been on their 'H' list."

11 *Well-Known Cheeses*

Of the many different cheeses made in Wisconsin, several deserve special mention. Some discussed here have long histories in Wisconsin. Two cheeses, Colby and brick, are Wisconsin originals—they were developed by cheese makers in this state.

Colby Cheese

Colby is named after the community in which it was developed—Colby, Wisconsin. It is a popular cheese with a golden color. Colby tastes and looks somewhat like cheddar, but is softer, more open-textured, and more elastic.

The village of Colby straddles the Marathon and Clark county line, in the north-central part of the state. From Civil War days until the 1880s, this part of Wisconsin was the land of the lumbermen, whose axes took down the giant pine forests. After the pines were removed, dairy farmers moved in.

Ambrose and Susan Steinwand moved to Clark County in 1877 from Manitowoc. They purchased 160 acres of land in Colby Township, about one and a half miles from the village of Colby. Steinwand cleared the land and began dairy farming. He decided to build a cheese factory, too. The building was twenty-four feet by thirty-six feet with a twelve-foot by twenty-foot addition. The Steinwand factory opened in 1882 with a party for the community. The *Colby Phonograph* on May 31, 1882, reported: "The best and the pleasantest dance ever held in Colby was the one at Steinwand Brothers Cheese Factory held last Monday evening. There was

*Making wooden
cheese tubs out of
imported willow
bands. Carl Marty
Company, 1938.*

*—From Historic
Cheesemaking Center.*

plenty of dancing, and to eat and drink, and all present seemed intent only on one thing, that was to enjoy themselves as much as possible. If the Steinwands make as much cheese as we all had fun, their success is assured."[1] The Steinwand cheese factory produced about 125 pounds of cheese per day. Milk was delivered to the factory on stoneboats (a wooden implement used for removing stones from fields) pulled by oxen. Like other cheese factories in the state, Steinwand's factory operated only from early spring to late fall.

Exactly how the first Colby cheese was created remains a mystery. The most popular story claims that Joseph Steinwand, Ambrose's son, developed Colby cheese in 1885. As the story goes, young Steinwand was interested in developing a new kind of cheese. One day he was making a vat of cheddar, and it wasn't going well. In order to save the cheese, Joseph added an extra step

1. *Colby Cheese Centennial Souvenir Edition, Colby Chronicle,* July 12, 1983.

to the process, which involved washing the curd with cold water and then draining it off. This produced a cheese that was more moist and open-textured than cheddar. He decided to name this new cheese after the nearby village of Colby. Soon Colby cheese was widely known and enjoyed by those who wanted a semisoft cheese. And the village of Colby, Wisconsin, found a place in history.

Over the years, area cheese makers and historians have debated how the "accident" might have occurred. Some believe that the story may be more legend than fact. Some nonbelievers argue that Joseph Steinwand really learned the process for making Colby cheese from Lawrence Wertz, a Calumet County cheese maker. Others argue that the Colby cheese that Steinwand made wasn't the same Colby cheese we know today. Some say Steinwand made two kinds of Colby, a high-moisture variety for local consumption and a low-moisture variety for shipping outside of the region.[2]

No matter. Colby cheese became popular and remains so.

Colby is Colby because of the way it is made. Making Colby cheese does not involve the "cheddaring" process, during which slabs of curd are turned periodically before they are milled. When making Colby, the curd is cut, stirred, and heated (as it is with cheddar); then the whey is drained to the level of the curd. After that, cool water (about sixty degrees) is added, and the mix is stirred for several minutes. The curd is pushed to the sides of the vat, and the whey is drained. Salt is added, and the curd is placed in hoops and pressed. The cool water slows down fermentation and gas formation, and gives Colby its mild flavor.

Some cheese makers prefer making Colby cheese to making cheddar because it involves less work.

Brick Cheese

Brick cheese is also a Wisconsin original. The cheese is ivory to creamy yellow in appearance and has a smooth, open texture. The U.S. Department of Agriculture describes brick as "a sweet-curd, semisoft, cow's-milk cheese, with a mild but rather pungent and sweet flavor, midway between cheddar and Limburger but not so sharp as cheddar and not so strong as Limburger. The body is

---

2. Peter Weinschenk, "New light on Colby cheese history," in *Colby Chronicle*, 2.

softer than cheddar but firmer than Limburger, is elastic, and slices well without crumbling."[3]

John Jossi, a Swiss-born cheese maker who operated a cheese factory in Dodge County, developed brick cheese. In 1865, Jossi settled on a farm near the unincorporated community of Richwood, about three miles northeast of Watertown, and operated a Limburger cheese factory there. In 1875, he developed a process for making brick cheese and opened the first brick cheese factory in the United States about eight miles northeast of Watertown. This factory, like many others, was a family operation, with living quarters upstairs and the cheese-making and curing facilities in the basement. The basement was built into a hillside so that it was naturally cooler, and a good place for curing cheese. The factory operated until the end of 1943. Jossi opened several other brick cheese factories in Dodge and Jefferson Counties.

Roland Behle, a retired Dodge County cheese maker, is trying to elicit support for erecting a marker recognizing the Jossi brick cheese factory as the first in the nation.[4]

Today, brick cheese is made in six- or ten-pound loaves. Joe Widmer, who operates a cheese factory in Theresa in Dodge County said, "To make brick cheese, we dip the cheese into whey every day for two weeks, then wrap it in foil. After three weeks it smells. You can't make good stinky cheese, though, unless you start out with the best milk.

"Germans like brick cheese with beer," Widmer went on. "Before the refrigerator was invented, they kept brick cheese in a crock in the basement. Today we have refrigerators, and the cheese is put in with other foods. But sometimes, wives won't let their husbands have brick cheese because it smells up the refrigerator."[5]

How was brick cheese named? Some believe it refers to the shape of the finished product—the shape of a brick. Others claim

---

3. George P. Sanders, *Cheese Varieties and Descriptions*, U.S. Department of Agriculture, Agricultural Handbook No. 54 (Washington, D.C., 1953), 16.

4. Gloria Hafemeister, "Cheesemaker recalls the rich tradition of his family," *Watertown Daily Times*, April 6, 1996.

5. Gloria Hafemeister, "Fourth-graders learn cheese making in Theresa factory," *Wisconsin State Farmer*, May 1996.

that early cheese makers used bricks to press the moisture from the cheese.

Cheddar Cheese

When most people say cheese, they mean cheddar. It is the most popular cheese in the world. About half of the cheese made in Wisconsin today is cheddar cheese.

Cheddar cheese takes its name from the village of Cheddar in Somersetshire, England, where it was first made in the 1500s. Kitchen cheese, made by dairy wives in this country before cheese factories were established, was a type of cheddar. The first cheese factory in the United States made cheddar cheese.

For a description of the cheddar-making process, see Chapter 7, "How Cheese Is Made."

Today, cheddar cheese is made in several wholesale sizes. "Mammoths" are the largest cheddars. They are cylindrical and may weigh between seventy-five pounds and 12,000 pounds. Cheddar is also made in 500-pound barrels and 640-pound blocks and in an assortment of smaller sizes and shapes including:

More than 30 percent of all the cheese produced in the United States comes from Wisconsin.

- Longhorn: 12-pound cylinder, 6 inches in diameter and 13 inches long.
- Flat: 35-pound cylinder, 15 inches in diameter and 7 inches thick.
- Daisy: 22-pound cylinder, 13 inches in diameter and 6 inches thick.
- Midget: 15-pound cylinder, 10 inches in diameter and 5 inches thick.
- Favorite: 5-pound cylinder, 7 inches in diameter and 4 inches thick.
- Block: 40-pound rectangle, 7 1/4 inches wide, 11 1/2 inches high, and 14 1/2 inches long.
- Loaf: 5-pound rectangle, 3 1/2 inches wide, 3 1/2 inches high, and 11 1/2 inches long.

The largest cheddar cheese, called "Belle of Wisconsin," was made by Simon's Specialty Cheese in Little Chute in 1988. It weighed 40,000 pounds and is listed in the 1994 *Guinness Book of World Records*. An expert cheese-making team, using 400,000 pounds of fresh milk, worked twenty-four hours straight to

Art and Fritz Escher lifting a cloth holding Swiss cheese curds, as Walt Etter watches. Monticello North Side Swiss Cheese Factory, Green County, c. 1940.

—From Connie Halverson.

produce the giant cheese. Belle of Wisconsin toured the United States for more than two years in a sixty-foot, glass-walled refrigerated trailer, its temperature computer-controlled to maintain ideal conditions for aging. At the end of the tour, the cheese was graded as Grade A Cheddar. The cheese was then cut into one-pound pieces and sold as premium aged Wisconsin cheddar.

Swiss Cheese

Swiss cheese (also called Emmentaler) is a firm, ivory-colored cheese with a mellow, nutty taste. It is best known for its holes, some as large as a quarter.

The first question everyone asks is, How do the holes get there? Far-fetched answers are offered: An elephant shot peanuts into the cheese. Mice ate out the holes.

Cheese maker John Bussman recalls stopping in a Lafayette County tavern one day and having the bartender ask him how the holes got in the Swiss cheese. Bussman began giving a scientific answer when a customer, with a big smile on his face, interrupted. "They don't put the holes in the Swiss cheese," he said. "They put the cheese around the holes."

In fact, the holes are formed by the action of special bacteria, which are included in the mix of starter bacteria that is added to the milk. The holes form in the cheese as it ages. Many cheese makers believe that Swiss is one of the most difficult cheeses to make.

Many people associate Swiss cheese with Green County, and well they should. Between the 1920s and 1950s, Monroe, the county seat, was known as the Swiss Cheese Capital of the World. Nicholas Gerber is credited with starting the first Swiss cheese factory in Washington Township in Green County in 1869. It was on the Dietrich Freitag farm, about a mile and half north of Monticello.

For many years, Swiss cheese was made in round copper kettles, not rectangular vats. The kettles came in various sizes; the most commonly used kettle in Wisconsin was five feet in diameter. These held 2,000 pounds of milk and more. A cheese wheel weighing between 185 and 200 pounds could be made from a 2,000-pound kettle of milk.

Swiss cheese was made from raw, unpasteurized milk, with a fat content of three to three and a half percent. In later years, the milk was sometimes heat-treated.

When the curd was firm enough to cut, a curd cutter called a Swiss cheese harp was moved from back to front and side to side in the kettle, forming rectangular strips. Cutting and stirring continued until the curds were cut into pieces about one-eighth inch square. The cheese curds were then stirred for fifteen minutes to a half-hour; this step was called foreworking. After this, the curds were heated to a temperature of about 120 to 130 degrees while they were continuously stirred. This heating and stirring went on from about a half-hour to an hour.

Next, the curd was enclosed in a coarsely woven dipping cloth, which was slid under the curd. The dipping cloth was wrapped around a flat piece of flexible steel, one-half inch wide and long enough to reach beyond the lips of the kettle. It was a considerable art to slip the dipping cloth under the curd, following the curvature of the kettle. And the 120-degree-plus temperature of the whey could be quite uncomfortable. Novice cheese makers often thrust their arms into cold water just before immersing them in the kettle. To commence the process, the cheese maker put two corners of the dipping cloth in his mouth. Then he worked the rest of the dipping cloth under the curd until he could grab the remaining two corners as they unwound from the flexible metal bar. With a block and tackle, the cloth full of curd was lifted above the kettle, and the excess whey was allowed to drain into the kettle. The sack of curd at this point weighed well over 250 pounds. The bag of curd was then lowered into a circular wooden or stainless-steel hoop.

With a deft maneuver, the cheese maker removed the dipping cloth from the cheese and replaced it with a specially designed piece of cheesecloth and burlap. He did this quickly, to assure that the cheese did not lose its shape while it was out of the hoop. The cheese was then placed on a press lid, which in the early days was a wooden circle that was larger than the cheese hoop and enclosed the cheese. Another press lid was placed on top of the cheese. With a specially designed cheese press—some were made of one-half of an old truck spring—the cheese was gently pressed to remove excess whey. Press lids were usually thirty-six inches in diameter; an unused one weighed nearly fifty pounds. As they were used, they absorbed moisture from the cheese and became much heavier. The weight included the iron band around it. After about two hours of pressing, the cheese was turned and the cheesecloth replaced, and the cheese was pressed for two more hours. The third time it was turned, the cheese was placed on cheesecloth that was especially flat, so no wrinkles formed in the cheese. Wrinkles could cause splits in the cheese while it was curing in the cellar—a defect to be avoided.

A Swiss cheese harp plays no music. It was used to cut cheese curds during the making of Swiss cheese.

Swiss cheese makers disagreed on how many times cheese should be turned and pressed. One old cheese maker said, "You keep turning the cheese, and the whey keeps going to the middle." Turning and pressing was stopped when no more whey drained from the cheese.

During the pressing process, some cheese oozed out around the form. Old-time cheese makers used a sharpened tablespoon that they ran around the form to remove this excess cheese. They also tapped the tablespoon on top of the cheese to detect whey pockets.

Generally, the morning after the cheese was made, it was taken to a cold room (about fifty-five degrees) where it was salted in a brine tank. Depending on how much rind formation was desired, the cheese was salted for two or three days. Then the wheel of

A young Swiss cheese maker, John Bussman, showing off his muscles. Swiss cheese makers washed 200-pound wheels of cheese by hand and moved them from shelf to shelf while the cheese was curing. Many of these cheese makers weighed only 125 to 150 pounds but could lift far more than their weight.

—From John Bussman.

cheese was placed on a shelf in a curing room (sixty-five to seventy-two degrees) where the cheese maker washed it with salty water and turned it every few days.[6]

Handling 200-pound cheese wheels was no small task. Cheese maker Jeff Wideman said, "Washing cheese wheels is an art. A small man could handle those big wheels if he knew how to do it. You used the weight of the cheese to your advantage. In the storage room we had shelves eight high. We'd wash the wheels on the second shelf and lift them to the fifth shelf. The fifth shelf was even with my nose. Standing on a box, we'd wash those wheels on the fifth shelf and lift them to the eighth shelf. We'd leave the bottom shelf open for the cheese to cool down a little. One day we had a little too much milk in a kettle. The wheel weighed 256

---

6. The description of the Swiss cheese-making process is from the author's conversation with John Bussman.

Wheels of Swiss cheese were shipped in wooden boxes. Carl Marty Company, Green County, 1938.

—From Historic Cheesemaking Center.

pounds. Last man to the cellar had that big one to wash. Better not be late."[7]

John Bussman said cheese wheels were handled this way: "You'd cup it with your hands and bring it down to here [belt level]. Then you've got it, and you'd roll it on the table called a 'bock.' If you were short, it was more of a challenge. I had the height. Did Swiss cheese makers have bad backs? A lot of them did."

The wheels were handled many times before the cheese was ready for sale. As Bussman explained, "We'd wash and restack the cheese two or three times a week, depending on how much mold developed on the outside." Each time the cheese was washed and turned, it was placed on a clean cheese lid, to help prevent excessive mold formation. Used cheese lids were washed in preparation for reuse. Washing lids was a task often relegated to the younger of the cheese maker's children.

The eyes began to form when the cheese was about three weeks old. The old-time Swiss-cheese makers thumped on the cheese with their finger, listening to the sound. They would place the first finger of their right hand over the second finger, then allow the first finger to slip back toward the thumb. As the holes formed, the

---

7. From a 1995 videotaped interview, on file with the Historic Cheesemaking Center, Monroe, WI.

cheese wheels made a different sound than before. After four to six weeks, they were returned to the cold room (about forty to fifty-five degrees) until they were graded or shipped to a wholesaler for grading.

One of the challenges of making Swiss cheese was waiting for three to five weeks to see if the process was working. If the cheese was bad, the cheese maker often faced going out of business. As a retired cheese maker told me, "Some cheese factories burned because they were 'struck by lightning,' but no one would admit the destroyed factory was full of bad cheese. It was a way to beat the problem."

Today, most Swiss cheese is made in rectangular vats, similar to those used for making other types of cheese. Rindless Swiss cheese blocks result from this process.

The largest producer of Swiss cheese in Wisconsin is the Waterford Food Products Company in New London, in Waupaca County. It is housed in a former powdered milk plant that was converted to Swiss cheese production.

Limburger Cheese

No cheese has more fun poked at it than Limburger. Once an extremely popular cheese in Wisconsin, it is, as John Luchsinger put it in 1880, "a premeditated outrage on the organs of smell."

Limburger is a semisoft, surface-ripened cheese that was first made in the Province of Luttich, Belgium. It is named for Limburg, in northeast Belgium, where much of it was marketed. Limburger cheese has a rind that varies in color from yellow to reddish-yellow.

Limburger cheese attains its characteristic taste and smell from a bacterial smear that is rubbed on the outside of the cheese several times while it is curing. Myron Olson, manager of the Chalet Cheese Cooperative near Monroe, called this cloudy mix of water, salt, and proprietary bacteria, "schmier." In just a few days, the smeared cheese changes from white to a golden color. Olson said that after about two months the cheese develops a sweet taste. After three or four months, its taste reaches its peak.[8] The cheese ripens from the outside in, and when ready for marketing, is sold in seven- to eight-ounce packages.

8. Patricia Gadsby, "Light Elements: Why Mosquitoes Suck," *Discover*, August 1997, 45.

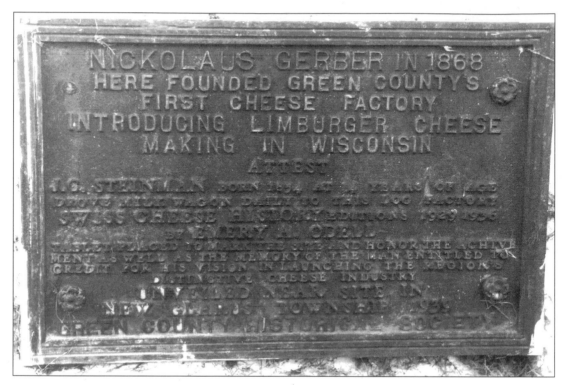

NICKOLAUS GERBER IN 1868
HERE FOUNDED GREEN COUNTY'S
FIRST CHEESE FACTORY
INTRODUCING LIMBURGER CHEESE
MAKING IN WISCONSIN

Located four miles southwest of New Glarus in Green County, this plaque marks the place where Nicholas Gerber established Green County's first cheese factory in 1868. Gerber made Limburger cheese.

Rudolph Benkert, a Swiss immigrant, who came to Green County in 1867, began making small amounts of Limburger cheese that year. He made what was known as experimental Limburger and cured it in the cellar of his home.[9]

Nicholas Gerber, a native of Canton Bern in Switzerland, is credited with establishing the first Green County Limburger cheese factory, in 1868 on the Albert Babler Farm, four miles southwest of New Glarus.[10] (A year later he started what is credited to be the first Swiss cheese factory in the county.) This early factory operated in a log house. The cheese cellar was built back into the hill behind the Babler farm. Mr. Babler and five or six other farmers delivered milk to the factory during its the first season.[11]

By 1925, Green County was producing 4.2 million pounds of Limburger cheese, nearly all of the Limburger made in the United States.[12] At one time, the Swiss cheese factories of Green County

9. Odell, *Swiss Cheese Industry*, 8.

10. E. C. Hamilton, *The Story of Monroe* (Monroe, WI: Monroe Public Schools, 1976), 107.

11. Odell, *Swiss Cheese Industry*, 23-24.

12. Ibid., 27.

made more Limburger cheese than Swiss cheese. Today, the only cheese factory in the United States making Limburger is the Chalet Cheese Cooperative near Monroe in Green County.

At one time, Limburger cheese was served in taverns with dark bread and onions. When Prohibition went into effect in 1919, the market for Limburger cheese plummeted. C. J. Kremer, the Dairy and Food Commissioner of Wisconsin in 1928, reported, "The Limburger cheese industry was on a fair way to complete passing out. With the closing of the saloons the sale of Limburger gradually declined until it almost reached the finishing point.... There appeared a surplus of Limburger cheese in the latter part of 1924 and 1925 which became too hard and too strong for sale in its original form." The commissioner went on to describe how Limburger cheese makers learned to package Limburger in a new way, so that the cheese didn't smell until the package was opened. He ended his comments with, "...people of all races are again eating Limburger cheese in this form. The manufacture of Limburger cheese in the past three years has been perhaps one of the most profitable to the farmers because of this fact."[13]

The people of Green County are proud of their Swiss and Limburger cheese heritage. In a 1954 county atlas, an enthusiastic writer said,

> Here is the greatest Swiss and Limburger cheese producing area in the United States. Endowed with water from limestone sources, Green County has what it takes to grow the lush feed needed for the cheese-industry milch [milk] cows. Here are some of the nation's choicest herds—and some of the nature's choicest scenery.
>
> Cheese three times a day is enjoyed by many Green County citizens. Yes, Limburger as a breakfast delicacy is not uncommon. Remember that Green County cheese is just about the last word in flavor and texture, and that the population is predominately native-born Swiss or of Swiss descent.... Colorful old-world customs and costumes remain. The people themselves are industrious, thrifty, friendly. As cheese makers they work in the grand old

---

13. C. J. Kremer, *Biennial Report of the Dairy and Food Commissioner of Wisconsin* (Madison, WI: Office of the Dairy and Food Commissioner, 1928), 114.

tradition of quality. When they play, their laughter and songs echo across the green valleys."[14]

Stories about Limburger cheese abound. Kim Tschudy shared the following from the July 6, 1887, edition of the *Monroe Sentinel:* "While loading cheese one day last week, Fred Gerber was thrown from the wagon to the ground, resulting in the fracture of a shoulder blade. Had the cheese been Limburger, its enormous strength would no doubt have killed him instantly."

John Bussman told a story about a Swiss fellow who had been a cheese maker before World War II. When the fellow came home from the war, he decided to try something different, so he moved to Arkansas to work in the poultry business. One day he visited the local grocery store in Arkansas and asked for Limburger cheese.

"Nope, haven't got any," replied the storekeeper. "But I've got a truck that goes up to Wisconsin once in a while. I'll ask the driver to haul some Limburger cheese back for you. I'll let you know when it comes."

A month went by and then six weeks. The fellow decided to stop by the grocery store to see if his Limburger cheese had come in.

"Say, did you ever get that Limburger cheese I ordered?" he asked.

"Ya, it came," the grocery man answered. "In fact I ordered it twice, and it came twice. It was spoiled both times; it smelled awful. I had to throw it out."

Even in Monroe, which was to become the Limburger center of the nation, the prejudice against the smelly cheese was considerable. Some of the farmers who had come to the area from the East refused to take their milk to a Limburger factory. Emory Odell reports in his book on cheese making that "school children along the road pinched their noses as the Limburger wagons passed on their way to Monroe. It is said that at one time an ordinance was proposed in the city council to keep Limburger hauling off the main streets because the odor was so offensive. As it became realized that Limburger was an important commodity of trade the cheese became more respected."[15] In Monroe, the smell of money became more powerful than the smell of the cheese.

---

14. *Pictorial County Atlas: Green County, Wisconsin* (Chicago, IL: The Loree Co., 1954), 3.

15. Odell, *Swiss Cheese Industry*, 18.

Carol Tourdot holding Limburger cheese. Chalet Cheese Cooperative, Monroe.

In 1935, a Limburger "trial" took place. It all started when a rural mail carrier in Iowa claimed he'd gotten ill from the smell of a package containing Limburger cheese. Warren F. Miller, the acting postmaster of Independence, Iowa, pulled out an old regulation that specifically barred Limburger cheese from being sent through the mail.

John J. Burkhard, Monroe's postmaster, challenged the postal department's rules and even forwarded a cake of the offending Limburger for the department to consider. The postal authorities handled the matter very delicately, finally ruling that Limburger could be mailed if the odor was suppressed.

But someone in Iowa once again smelled out a parcel of Limburger, and the debate continued. Monroe's postmaster accused the Iowa people of lacking "an appreciation of Limburger's esthetic value." The Wisconsin postmaster said, "Limburger creates its own exclusive atmosphere and asks no odds of anyone." He wrote the Iowa postmaster, "Green County folks do not judge books by their covers, people by faces, or good cheese by its smell." He ended his letter by challenging the Iowa postmaster to a "trial."

The event took place in March 1935 at the Julian Hotel in Dubuque, in the presence of the public and the press. Limburger was sniffed by all in attendance. The official judges for the event gave a unanimous nod to the cheese. News of the trial made its way to the Associated Press wire service, whose reports enhanced the sales of Green County Limburger cheese.

In 1935, the Monroe postmaster was chosen Cheese Day president. He invited his Iowa opponent to be a guest of honor at the celebration.[16]

A writer recently reported that Limburger cheese attracts mosquitoes. Mosquitoes had been placed in a small wind tunnel about five feet downwind from two traps; one contained Limburger cheese and the other fresh air. These discerning mosquitoes, knowing a good thing when they smelled it, had chosen Limburger cheese three times as often as the fresh air.[17]

Limburger attains its characteristic taste and smell from a bacterial smear that is rubbed on the outside of the cheese several times while it is curing.

Monterey Jack

Monterey Jack is a creamy white cheese, semisoft and less dense than cheddar. It has a delicate, buttery, slightly tart flavor. Monterey Jack may be additionally flavored with bacon, chives, dill, garlic, hot peppers, onion, or salsa. Sometimes cheese makers mix Monterey Jack with Colby cheese. Some call the mixture Colby-Jack. Monterey Jack is made in ten-pound wheels and blocks of various sizes.

Monterey Jack was first produced on farms in Monterey County, California, about 1892. It can be made from pasteurized whole, partly skimmed, or skim milk. The process of making Monterey Jack is similar to that of making Colby, but it takes less time.

Mozzarella

Pizza has become a standard food item for millions of people. Without mozzarella cheese, we would not have pizza as we know it. One of the important characteristics of mozzarella cheese is its ability to stretch without breaking. How many of us have picked up a piece of pizza and watched the cheese stretch from the pan to our mouths?

16. Ibid., 66-67.

17. Gadsby, "Light Elements," 44.

Today, most pizza cheese is a combination of whole-milk mozzarella, which has a creamy texture and melts and flows over the top of the pizza when it is heated, and part-skim mozzarella, which browns better and faster.

To assure that the cheese melts and stretches well, the mozzarella curd is heated, stretched, and kneaded into parallel strands. The curd is molded into blocks that range in size from five pounds to forty pounds, with eight-pound loaves being a popular size. The blocks are bathed in cold-water brine to firm them up; at the same time, some salt penetrates the cheese, which adds to its flavor and extends shelf life.

String Cheese

String cheese, which is becoming more and more popular as a snack food, is really not a separate kind of cheese. It is mozzarella cheese that is sold in one-ounce strands or ropes. Many people outside of Wisconsin are just becoming acquainted with string cheese. When they first buy it, they don't know how to eat it. Of course, you can eat string cheese by merely biting a chunk off the end of a strand. But then you miss the fun of pulling the strand apart and enjoying the individual strings.

Bulk milk trucks are used to pick up milk from farmers and deliver it to the cheese factory.

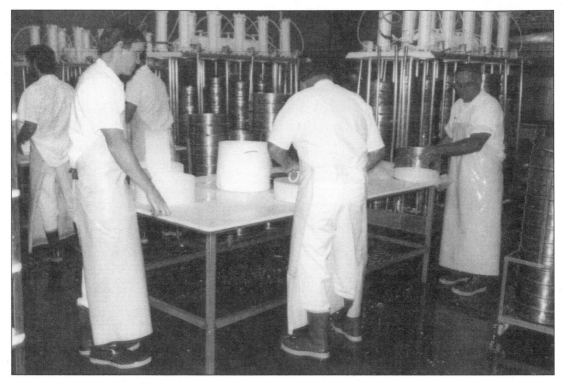

Parmesan cheese being removed from molds. Eau Galle Cheese Factory, Durand, 1996.

Parmesan

Parmesan is found in the grocery stores in a variety of forms: in blocks, shredded, and grated, the latter often in a shaker container—open it and you can sprinkle the cheese directly onto your spaghetti or salad. It's more fun, though, to take a piece of whole Parmesan and grate some long, fresh pieces onto your food.

During the production of Parmesan, curds are cut into pieces the size of kernels of corn. The curds are cooked in whey at higher temperatures than other cheeses, and the cheese is cured for ten months or more to achieve the full flavor and the granular texture.

EAU GALLE CHEESE FACTORY

PARMESAN
Made from pasteurized cultured milk, salt and enzymes.

715-283-4211
DURAND, WI 54736

SINCE 1945

12 *Specialty Cheeses*

Specialty cheeses began appearing regularly in delis, grocery stores, and food markets in the 1980s. Several characteristics differentiate them from more common cheeses, such as cheddar, Monterey Jack, and mozzarella. Most have their roots in other countries but are now made in Wisconsin. All are made in small amounts, especially when compared to cheddar and mozzarella, which are manufactured in the hundreds of millions of pounds. Sometimes a "regular" cheese becomes a specialty cheese when it is modified in some way. For instance, cheddar is considered a specialty cheese when hot peppers and bacon are added to it. In a few cases, cheeses that were once popular in Wisconsin, such as Limburger and Swiss made in large wheels, are now termed specialty cheeses because today they are made in small amounts.

In 1994, the Wisconsin Specialty Cheese Institute was founded as an extension of the Wisconsin Cheese Makers Association, to support and promote the development of specialized cheeses. Researchers there note that mozzarella was considered a specialty cheese thirty years ago. Thanks to pizza, mozzarella has become the second most popular cheese produced in Wisconsin. Other specialty cheeses are increasing in popularity as well. For instance, Wisconsin feta cheese production rose from 8.1 million pounds in 1993 to 14.6 million pounds in 1994. Gouda production increased from four million pounds in 1993 to 5.5 million pounds in 1994. Blue cheese production increased from 23 million pounds in 1990 to 30 million pounds in 1994.[1]

---

1. "Specialty Cheese Production: Wisconsin, 1993-1994," *Wisconsin 1995 Dairy Facts* (Madison, WI: Department of Agriculture, Trade, and Consumer Protection, 1995).

Specialty Cheese Plants

Between forty and fifty Wisconsin cheese plants make specialty cheeses. Many cheese industry people see the making of these cheeses as a way for small factories to survive among the giants in the business.

The Oak Grove Cheese Factory in Shawano County is an example. In the 1970s, Shawano County had seventeen cheese factories; now it has three. The Kust family, who operate the Oak Grove Cheese Factory, specialize by making Colby and cheddar longhorn cheeses, which are thirteen-pound cylinders. They flavor the cheese with onions, garlic, caraway, dill, peppers, and chives.[2]

Another example is the Springside Cheese Corporation in Oconto Falls, which makes about 15,000 pounds of various kinds of cheese daily from milk producers in Shawano, Oconto, and Marinette Counties. In addition to standard cheddar, Monterey Jack, and Colby, they make specialty cheeses: low-fat, low-salt, onion, garlic, and pepperjack cheese. They are considering making goat milk cheese.[3]

The Specialty Cheese Company in Lowell makes a variety of specialty cheeses, including Middle Eastern-style, Indian and Hispanic cheeses.

Organic Cheese

Raw milk cheese is made from milk that has not been pasteurized. It must be aged a minimum of sixty days.

Organic cheese, a type of specialty cheese, is gaining in popularity. A major producer of organic cheese in Wisconsin is the Coulee Region Organic Produce Pool (CROPP). Their brand name is Organic Valley. A cooperative headquartered in La Farge, CROPP represents a family of farms dedicated to supporting sustainable farming practices. They are affiliated with the National Farmers Organization.

CROPP's administrative and cheese-packaging operations are housed in a cheese factory that closed several years ago. Eighty-two organic farmers are members of the cooperative. They meet a strict set of standards for certification as organic farmers. They must not use chemicals on crop land for three years; they must have cows that are free of trace antibiotics and other drugs; they

---

2. "Oak Grove Cheese concentrates on specialty products," *The Country Today*, November 6, 1996.

3. "Company considers adding goat cheese to production line," *The Country Today*, October 30, 1996.

Louise Hemstead, operations manager for CROPP, observes organic cheese packaging at the cooperative's warehouse in La Farge, 1996

must not use BST (BGH) or other hormones to enhance milk production; and they must process and package dairy products according to strict guidelines.

CROPP began in 1987 with seven farmers who raised organic vegetables for the Chicago market. Some of the vegetable growers were dairy farmers, and a year later they began producing organic milk. Soon dairy sales overshadowed the vegetable business. Vegetables now comprise about one percent of sales. At first, the co-op made cheddar cheese. By 1990, they were making mozzarella, which is now their number-one seller. Today, CROPP makes twenty-two cheeses, from both raw and pasteurized milk.

Twenty dairy plants make organic cheese, butter, and other dairy products for the co-op. Louise Hemstead, operations manager, said, "Rather than trying to build our own cheese plant, we are helping some of the existing plants. It's a great relationship for all parties. The cheese factories don't have their money tied up in the milk. They don't have to pay for our milk. They get paid for their labor as soon as they ship the cheese over here."

CROPP is always concerned that members follow the rules for producing organic milk. They are also concerned that cheese plants making their organic cheese keep organic milk separate from regular milk. To do this, Hemstead explained, each milk hauler keeps a careful record of the number of pounds of organic milk picked up from each organic farmer. Upon arrival at the cheese plant, organic milk is stored in separate silos. When cheese-making operations begin, organic milk passes through the pasteurizer ahead of any regular milk the plant may be processing. Organic cheese is tracked carefully throughout the cheese-making process and is always kept separate from regular cheese. One important difference in making organic cheese is that the process avoids animal-based rennet and laboratory-created gene-spliced coagulants.

The co-op owns one truck and contracts with five other haulers to pick up milk from organic producers. These haulers may haul conventional milk after or before they haul organic milk, but they always wash their tank trucks between loads.

An Organic Valley sign greets visitors to the cooperative, which has headquarters in La Farge, 1996. CROPP is devoted to producing organic dairy products as well as organic vegetables.

The co-op works with several markets, including the multistate Whole Foods chain. They employ fifty-two people, who cut, package, market, and do administrative work. Sales for all their organic dairy products were about $13.5 million in 1996. Sales for 1997 were about $21 million.

Other Specialty Cheeses Made in Wisconsin

Differences among various specialty cheeses are accounted for by factors such as the kind of milk used (unpasteurized cow's milk, organic milk, goat's milk, sheep's milk), and variances in the manufacturing process: the kind of bacteria introduced into the milk, temperature for cooking the curds and whey, how finely the curd is cut, salting approaches, the shape and size of molds into which the cheese is placed, whether or not the cheese is rubbed with bacteria, and how long the cheese is aged.[4]

Ackawi: Originally from Lebanon and Syria, ackawi (ah-cow'-ee) is a soft, white cheese with a smooth texture, a mild taste, and no acidity. It is made from cow's milk and is prepared in brine to

---

4. Except where noted, information on specialty cheeses is taken from the *Wisconsin Cheesecylopedia*, and Sanders, *Cheese Varieties and Descriptions.*

produce its characteristic salty taste. Ackawi works well as a snack or even as a light meal on its own. Many like it as a side dish with a salad or with cucumber rounds.

Asiago: Asiago (ah-see-ah'-go) is a pale yellow Italian cheese that is available fresh, medium, or aged. Fresh Asiago has a clean, mild flavor and a soft texture. Medium Asiago has a more intense flavor and is firm and somewhat granular. Aged Asiago has a buttery, nutty taste—some say its taste is a cross between white cheddar and Parmesan—and a hard, granular texture. The color of the wax on Asiago indicates its flavor. Clear or white wax means the cheese is mild; brown suggests medium; and black indicates aged.

A key step in making Asiago cheese is continuous cutting and heating of the curd until particles are the size of wheat grains. Once the particles are this size, they are pressed in hoops. The cheese is then salted in a brine bath and cured on shelves for sixty days or more.

In the dairy case, Asiago is usually available as a wedge cut from a wheel. Fresh Asiago can be eaten as table cheese and on sandwiches. The medium and aged varieties are great in soups, sauces, salads, salad dressings, garnishes, and casseroles.

Baby Swiss: Baby Swiss was developed in this country. It is not aged as long as traditional Swiss, has smaller holes, and is usually produced in smaller sizes. It is pale yellow in color with a soft, silky texture and a mild, buttery, creamy taste. Baby Swiss does not have the characteristic "bite" of traditional Swiss. It's a favorite cheese for soups, sauces, fondues, salads, sandwiches, and casseroles. Some Baby Swiss is also smoked. In the dairy counter, it is usually found as wedges cut from wheels or chunks cut from bulk loaves.

Blue Cheese and Gorgonzola: Blue cheese and Gorgonzola (gohr-gohn-zoh'-lah) are creamy cheeses, ivory in color with blue-gray veins. Blue (*bleu* in French) comes from France; Gorgonzola has an Italian heritage. Molds create the earthy flavor. Blue cheese is dry and crumbly; Gorgonzola is dry and more crumbly.

Making blue cheese involves several steps that are quite different from those taken in the cheddar-making process. A blue-green mold (*penicillium roqueforti*) is added to the milk when it is in the

Block Swiss cheese floating in salt brine, an important step when making Swiss cheese. Prima Käse cheese factory, Monticello, 1997.

—Photo by Steve Apps.

vat. Later, after the curd is formed, the whey is drained, and the curd is dipped out of the vat by hand. The curd is not pressed, but is placed in eight-inch stainless-steel cylinders that hold about six and a half pounds of cheese. The cylinders are turned about every half hour. The following morning, the cheese is removed from the cylinders and put in a salt brine, where it remains for three days. After it is removed from the salt brine, it is allowed to dry. A special product, Delvocid, is rubbed on the cheese to prevent mold from forming on the outside.

The cheese is next placed in plastic bags. The following step is the key to making blue cheese. A special machine with fifty-six needles on each side punches holes in the cheese. This allows air to enter and mold to grow—the bluish-green mold that gives the cheese its distinct color and flavor. The holes also allow the carbon dioxide that is produced by the mold to escape. This process takes place in a curing room, where the cheese is stored at a temperature of fifty to fifty-five degrees.

After thirty days, the cheese is placed in another curing room, where the temperature is maintained at thirty-eight to forty degrees for another thirty days. It is then cut and packaged.

Many steps for making Gorgonzola are similar to those for making blue cheese. One major difference is curing time. Minimum curing time for blue cheese is sixty days, and for Gorgonzola, ninety days, although some Gorgonzola is cured for up to a year.[5]

These cheeses are used in salads, soups, salad dressings, dips, and grilled sandwiches. They are available crumbled in packages, or may be purchased in wedges.

Brie and Camembert: Brie (bree) and Camembert (cam'-em-bear) are centuries-old creamy French cheeses, pale ivory in color and with a rich, earthy, mushroomlike flavor. During the production process, the surface of the cheese is sprayed with *penicillium candidum.* The taste of the cheese strengthens in flavor, and the beneficial mold develops into a distinctive, soft, velvety growth on the surface of the cheese that is known as bloomy rind. The flavors of these two cheeses are nearly identical, although some cheese tasters say Camembert is more intense. They are used for tortes, in soups and sauces, and as an appetizer. The cheeses come in eight-ounce wheels or four-ounce half-wheels.

The average person in the U.S. consumes about nine pounds of cheddar cheese per year and about ten pounds of mozzarella (mostly on pizzas).

Butterkäse: A semisoft cheese with a German heritage, Butterkäse (but'-er-cahs) is made with part-skim milk. It is aged about six weeks and is a mild-tasting cheese. Despite its name, Butterkäse is not made from, nor does it contain, butter. The cheese had a smooth body, a creamy texture, and small "eyes" or pinprick-sized holes. It is easy to slice for sandwiches, melts well over steamed vegetables, and makes a tasty snack that compliments fresh fruits. The cheese is sold in packaged wedges or chunks.

Cold-Pack Cheese: This cheese was developed by a Wisconsin tavern owner who wanted to provide his customers with a cheese that could be easily spread. Many taverns were called clubs, and this cheese became known as "club" or "crock" cheese. Cold-pack cheese is made from natural cheeses and is sometimes flavored with fruits, vegetables, meats, or spices.

5. The description of the process for making Gorgonzola and blue cheese is from the author's conversation with William Schrock, Salemville Cheese Cooperative, Cambria, WI.

Cold-pack cheese contains one or more kinds of cheeses, which are ground and mixed. Unlike Process cheese, cold-pack cheese is not heated. Thus, it must be refrigerated. Federal standards require that cold-pack cheese contain the same amount of moisture as the cheese from which it is made. Some variation is allowed when spices, meats, etc., are added.

Cold-pack cheese is a favorite cheese for parties, and is available in nut-covered loaves, cakes, logs, and balls. It is also sold in crocks, tubs, and cups.

Supposedly, early cheese makers shaped Edam into balls so they could roll them down the gangplanks into ships for export.

Edam: Edam (ee'-dahm) is a Dutch cheese with a light, buttery, nutty taste and a smooth but firm texture. Edam is typically made from part-skim milk, so it slices easily. When making Edam, the curd is cut into three-eighth-inch cubes, stirred, and heated to a temperature of ninety to ninety-five degrees. The cheese curd is pressed in molds, giving it the shape of a flattened ball. Edam is commonly available in two- and four-pound balls and eight-ounce wheels, and it can be sliced from a loaf.

Farmers: This popular cheese is cream colored, mild tasting, lower in fat, and often made in part from skim milk. There are no standards to define it, however. As one cheese maker said, "Farmers cheese is whatever the cheese maker wants it to be."

Feta: In Greece, feta (feh'-ta) cheese is made from sheep's or goat's milk. In Wisconsin, it is made from cow's milk. During the manufacturing process, the curd is cut into blocks and dry salt is rubbed on the surface. Feta is ready to eat in four or five days from the time the cheese-making process begins. Feta cheese is chalk white in color and has a firm, crumbly texture and a tart, salty taste. It is often flavored with black pepper, dill, garlic, jalapeño, or tomato. Feta is wonderful in salads, casseroles, stuffings, and stews. It can be purchased crumbled in eight- or sixteen-ounce cups, or in wrapped blocks.

Gouda: Gouda (goo'-dah) cheese, which originated in Holland, is smooth and creamy, with a light, buttery, somewhat nutty taste. Gouda is made in much the same way as Edam. The curd is heated to slightly higher temperatures (100 to 106 degrees), giving the cheese a firmer body and better keeping quality. The interior is pale yellow; the exterior may be covered with red wax, which suggests it is mild, or with a yellow or clear wax, which means it is aged. If it is covered with a black or brown wax, it is likely smoked. Gouda works well in soups, casseroles, and open-faced sandwiches. In the dairy case, Gouda is often available in eight-ounce wheels or as slices from a nine-pound wheel.

Havarti: Havarti (huh-var'-tee) is a pale-yellow cheese, with tiny holes, creamy texture, and a buttery, slightly acidic flavor. It is the Danish version of the more pungent German Tilsit cheese. The Center for Dairy Research at the University of Wisconsin-Madison has developed a Wisconsin-type Havarti that is firmer in texture and has a more buttery flavor than other types. It's a good cheese for sandwiches, casseroles, and fondues. It can be bought in sandwich-size chunks that have been cut from nine-pound loaves. Sometimes cheese makers flavor Havarti with such ingredients as dill, caraway, and hot peppers.

Mascarpone: Mascarpone (mass-car-po'-neh) is a white Italian cheese, thick and creamy in texture, with a rich, buttery, and slightly sweet flavor. It is a fresh cheese, which means it is not aged or cured to develop flavor. Its texture is like thick whipped cream. Mascarpone contains seventy percent milk fat and is thus known as a triple cream cheese. It is used in soups, sauces, desserts, tortes, spreads, and frostings, and is sold in cups ranging in size from four to sixteen ounces.

Muenster: Muenster (mun'-ster), which originated in France and Germany, was one of the first semisoft cheeses that European immigrants made in the late 1800s. The Wisconsin variety is somewhat milder than its European counterparts. It is a creamy white cheese with an orange or white surface, and a mild to mellow taste. The texture becomes creamier with age. The orange rind results after cheese makers dip the cheese in annatto, a harmless vegetable dye. Muenster is good in sandwiches but also may be used as a pizza topping or in casseroles. It can be purchased in wrapped chunks cut from loaves or five-pound wheels.

Neufchatel: Neufchatel (nuf'-sha-tel) is a French cheese that resembles cream cheese but contains more moisture and less fat.

During the cheese-making process, the curd is stirred, rather than cut, until it is smooth. The cheese is creamy white with a smooth texture and a rich, nutty, slightly sweet flavor. It is softer than cream cheese. Neufchatel is used in spreads, dips, baked goods, and frostings. It is generally available in three- or eight-ounce packages.

Paneer: From India, paneer (pah-near') is a mild, low-acid white cheese similar to cottage cheese. It is made by curdling milk, then drawing off the liquid. Paneer is traditionally used in curry dishes. It also goes well with sliced cucumbers or watermelon wedges.

Process cheese: Process cheese is a family of cheeses available in individually wrapped slices, and in loaves, squeeze bottles, jars, crocks, and tubs. The flavor of a Process cheese depends on the type of cheese from which it is made. Cheddar cheese is used most often, but Colby, Swiss, brick, Edam, Gouda, and other cheeses may be found in Process cheese.

Process cheese making begins with natural cheeses, which are trimmed, ground, and melted in steam-jacketed kettles. The federal Standards of Identity for Process cheese specify:

Annatto is a natural vegetable dye that gives cheddar and some other cheeses a yellow color. It is not a preservative and is tasteless.

- "Pasteurized Process Cheese." Contains no more than one percent additional moisture and no less fat than the legal limits for the natural cheese from which it is made.
- "Pasteurized Process Cheese Food." At least fifty-one percent of Pasteurized Cheese Food by weight must be cheese. Moisture minimum is twenty-three percent and maximum is forty-four percent. Dairy products such as cream, milk, whey, or concentrated mixtures of these may be added.
- "Pasteurized Process Cheese Spread." Requirements are similar to Pasteurized Process Cheese Food, but it must contain at least twenty percent fat, and the moisture must not exceed forty-four percent or be less than twenty-three percent.

For all Process cheeses, moisture and fat levels may vary slightly when fruits, vegetables, meats, or spices are added.

As novel as some of the Process cheeses are, Process cheese itself is not new. Cheese was heated and preserved in cans in Germany and Switzerland as early as 1895, and hard-ripened Process cheese was made in Switzerland in 1911. The United

Sweet Swiss cheese in the aging room. Prima Käse cheese factory, Monticello, 1997.

—Photo by Steve Apps.

States issued its first patent for Process cheese in 1916. An advantage of Process cheese historically was that it did not require refrigeration. Today its attraction is convenience.

Provolone: Provolone (pro-vo-lo′-neh) is a firm Italian cheese that becomes more granular with age. It is made by heating, stretching, and then molding the curd. It is a fun cheese to buy because it comes in the shape of a salami with a stout string tied around it lengthwise and several times around the middle. Sometimes it is available in the shape of a bell, a pear, or a ball. Provolone is a good cheese for salads, sandwiches, and pizza.

Queso blanco: Queso blanco (kay′-so blahn′-ko) is a soft white Hispanic cheese made from whole, partly skimmed, or skim milk. When making this cheese, the curd traditionally is broken up by hand and gently squeezed in the whey until firm. After about fifteen minutes, the whey is drained and the curd is further broken up, kneaded, and salted. Queso blanco can be eaten within a day or two after it is made, either without being pressed or after pressing. Some of the pressed cheeses can be stored up to two months.

Ricotta: Ricotta (re-caht′-ah) is an Italian cheese, originally made from whey left over from the making of mozzarella and Provolone. Today Wisconsin cheese makers make ricotta cheese from whole milk or part-skim milk, as well as from whey. It is a fresh cheese (in the same family as cottage cheese, cream cheese,

Block Swiss cheese produced by the Prima Käse cheese factory, Monticello, 1997.

—*Photo by Steve Apps.*

and Mascarpone), white, with a mild flavor and a texture that is creamy yet slightly grainy. It is good for stuffings and casseroles, and is available in cups ranging from four ounces to sixteen ounces.

Romano: Romano (ro-mah'-no) is a white Italian cheese that is hard and granular and has a sharp flavor. While many traditional Italian cheese makers make Romano from sheep's milk, Wisconsin cheese makers use cow's milk. During the cheese-making process, the cheese is pressed, removed from the hoops, and then immersed in a salt brine for several hours. The cheese is cured for not less than five months. Romano is grated or shaved on salads, goes well in soups and sauces, and may be used as a garnish. Look for slices of Romano in the dairy case, or in shakers of various sizes.

13 *Celebrating and Promoting Cheese*

Wisconsin people like a good party and celebrating cheese is a good excuse for having one. But cheese celebrations are important for other reasons. They recognize Wisconsin's dairy heritage. They honor the visionaries who had the courage to lead Wisconsin from wheat growing to dairy farming. They salute the farmer and his family, who work 200 acres of land, milk cows twice a day, and are the heart and soul of the state's rural communities. Celebrating cheese means honoring the dairy cow, too, the unsung heroine who eats, drinks, and makes milk—thousands of pounds of it a year.

Monroe Cheese Days

One of the oldest and largest cheese celebrations in the country is Cheese Days, which is held in mid-September of even-numbered years in Monroe. Founded in 1914, this cheese festival grows larger each time it's held.

A newspaper reporter wrote this about the first festival:

The first Cheese Day was held Tuesday, October 28, 1914, for the purpose of advertising the city. The night before the event, 23 firemen and two meat cutters worked assembly-line style to make 13,000 cheese sandwiches for the event. They used a total of 7,000 pounds of Swiss, Limburger, brick and block cheeses.

The sandwiches were given away at each corner of the Square, which represented the four different types of cheese used. The Monroe Concert Band and the Orangeville Concert Band entertained the crowd, which was estimated between 3,000 to 4,000. At night, there was dancing at Turner Hall and fireworks.[1]

The following year, a parade, Swiss wrestling, and a circus were added. In 1916, the parade was two miles long, and the crowd swelled to 25,000 spectators. Monroe celebrated its fifth Cheese Day in 1923, having missed several years because of World War I. During that year's festival, Monroe was proclaimed to be the Swiss Cheese Capital of the World. Thirty thousand people attended. Seven bands provided music, and the parade had seventy-five floats.

A highlight of the October 2, 1928, Cheese Day was a film that included President Calvin Coolidge sampling Green County cheese. Upon tasting the cheese, Coolidge said, "It's fine." A small problem, however, occurred during the evening's dance in Turner Hall. Five hundred couples were doing a "stomp" dance, and the management feared the building would collapse. Emory A. Odell, editor of the local newspaper, was president of the 1923 and 1928 Cheese Days. "It is Green County's 'at home' day," he said of the celebration. "It is celebrated in honor of the outstanding industry of the Swiss cheese-country. It is done in the distinctive fashion of 'Little Switzerland' as a means of expressing civic pride in a notable dairying achievement."[2]

Because of the Depression, the celebration was not held for seven years. It returned in 1935, and was promoted with a Limburger-sniffing contest between the postmasters of Dubuque, Iowa, and Monroe (see Chapter 11 for details).

The event was again suspended during World War II and re-established in 1950. The tenth Cheese Day was celebrated in 1955 with a 125-unit parade and music by local Swiss entertainers. After another ten-year gap, the festival returned in 1965 and was expanded to two days. An estimated 125,000 people attended. The 1967 Cheese Days featured the University of Wisconsin marching band playing, "Come to Cheese Days." By the 1970s, Cheese Days was being held in September every other year. The 1990 festival

1. "Cheese Days," *The Monroe Times*, September 21, 1996.

2. Odell, *Swiss Cheese Industry*, 70.

Visitors attending Monroe Cheese Days, 1996. The event is held during even-numbered years on the Courthouse Square in Monroe.

included a 200-unit parade, elephant shows, Swiss wrestling, and a celebrity milking contest.[3]

Between 200,000 and 250,000 people attended the 1996 Cheese Days. More than 500 kids were in a children's parade. About 1,500 people toured area cheese factories and farms to see cheese being made. Cheese Days planners added a Swiss Folk Fair to teach visitors about the Swiss people. The fair included Swiss music, Swiss costuming, and discussions of Swiss culture.

The location of today's celebration is especially pleasing. Exhibits and activities are located around the square in downtown Monroe, with the county's imposing red brick courthouse in the middle. A highlight is the cheese-making demonstration, during which a 200-pound Swiss-cheese wheel is made in a copper kettle. The festival also presents visitors with an opportunity to taste cheese and enjoy an array of Swiss foods.

June Dairy Month

Wisconsin sets aside the entire month of June as a time to recognize and celebrate everything connected to dairying. Many counties hold on-the-farm dairy breakfasts for which people turn

3. Ibid.

out by the hundreds to feast on scrambled eggs, cheese, ice cream with freshly picked strawberries, and milk.

Madison hosts "Cows on the Concourse" on the first Saturday of June as part of the weekly farmers' market on the Capitol Square. The event features dairy cows from the UW College of Agricultural and Life Sciences. Milking demonstrations are held, and children may pet dairy calves. Visitors can buy slices from a huge cheese sandwich, sample various types of cheese, and enjoy other dairy products.

Little Chute, in northeastern Wisconsin, holds their Great Wisconsin Cheese Festival, with cheese tasting, a cheese parade, and a cheesecake baking contest, on Friday, Saturday, and Sunday of the first weekend in June. In northwestern Wisconsin, Clayton celebrates Cheese Days on Father's Day weekend. For details on these and other festivals, see *Wisconsin Food Festivals* by Terese Allen (Amherst Press, 1995).

Calvin Coolidge, president of the United States from 1923 to 1929, enjoyed fishing in northern Wisconsin, along with Green County's Swiss cheese.

—From Historic Cheesemaking Center.

State and County Fairs

The Wisconsin State Fair, held in Milwaukee each year in August, features many things cheesy, from the state's best dairy cattle to informative exhibits about cheese and cheese making. The Governor's Annual State Fair Cheese Competition and Sweepstakes is held during the fair; outstanding Wisconsin cheese and cheese makers are honored. The Agricultural Products Building displays many different kinds of cheese, and offers an opportunity to both buy and taste.

The county fair is a long-standing tradition in Wisconsin, with one or more county fairs held every weekend from spring to fall. County fairs all promote dairying and cheese. They are good places to see the state's best dairy cattle, all primped up for the show-ring judge, and also provide opportunities to taste and buy cheese.

International Dairy Exposition

The International Dairy Exposition, held each year in Madison, attracts dairy cattle exhibitors from around the world. Here is where the world's top dairy cattle are showcased. Visitors can also view what's new in dairy equipment, taste cheese, and participate in a host of related activities. Most of the events not only celebrate cheese and the dairy industry, but promote it.

Farm organizations such as the Farm Bureau, the National Farmers Organization, and the Farmers Union promote dairy products. So do such organizations as the Coulee Region Organic Produce Pool (CROPP).

American Dairy Association

In 1938, dairy promotion organizations in Iowa, Illinois, Minnesota, and Wisconsin came together to form the American Dairy Association (ADA). The ADA was a voluntary program, with farmer members contributing one-half of one percent of their milk checks to the organization. John Oncken was hired as ADA manager for Wisconsin in 1978. "My goal," he said, "was to sign up half of Wisconsin's dairy farmers as members." By 1983, some 20,000 dairy farmers had joined, providing an income to the organization of about $5 million per year.

Wisconsin's ADA members supported many dairy promotion activities, from dairy recipe contests to cooking demonstrations on

TV. Their objective was to increase consumption of dairy products, primarily through education. Oncken had also wanted to support the development of innovative ideas—new ways of making cheese, for example. But money was always in short supply in an organization composed of voluntary members.

Wisconsin Milk Marketing Board

As ADA grew, state agricultural organizations petitioned the Wisconsin Department of Agriculture to initiate a mandatory "check-off" system, which required all dairy farmers to contribute to dairy promotion. At this time, a decision was made to form a new organization to replace ADA. In 1983, the Wisconsin Milk Marketing Board (WMMB) was formed. ADA of Wisconsin ceased operations in December 1983 and turned its assets—an office building and some $4 million—over to the WMMB. This new organization was now charged with promoting and marketing Wisconsin's dairy products.

By mandate, the WMMB does not lobby for or against legislation, buy or sell dairy products, or try to influence milk prices or milk production levels. With headquarters in Madison, it operates under an elected board of twenty-five farmer-directors. The organization has a professional staff of fifty-four people who are responsible for coordinating and carrying out an array of programs. The 1996 budget was about $26.7 million, with sixty-nine percent going to marketing activities.

Establishing partnerships is key for the WMMB. They work with farmers and grassroots organizations, such as 4-H groups and county dairy groups, by assisting with funding, training, and promotional materials. They also work with processors, manufacturers, marketers, and food-service distributors. Other partners include food-service operators, chefs (WMMB provides recipes that include Wisconsin cheese), food processors, and retailers.

In addition, the WMMB works closely with other major dairy states, the Dairy Council of Wisconsin, the University of Wisconsin-Madison Center for Dairy Research, and Dairy Management, Inc. (a national promotion and research organization).[4]

---

4. Information on the Wisconsin Milk Marketing Board is from "I've Always Wondered About That: A collection of WMMB statements, positions and results, 1994-95 Edition" (Madison, WI: Wisconsin Milk Marketing Board), 1995, and the author's conversation with John Oncken.

Although the organization sometimes generates controversy among farmers (especially when milk prices are low), most farmers and cheese makers applaud WMMB's efforts. Cheese maker Joe Widmer is pleased with the assistance he gets from the WMMB. "We got into new stores by running demos, cost-shared by the WMMB. They helped us design new labels. We worked with them on a sweepstakes programs, they helped put us in contact with distributors, and cost-shared on a display cooler in our store. The help I get from them helps the Wisconsin farmer and my business. I appreciate having a place where I can call for advice, and I need to have customers in order to stay in business. If small companies like ours can stay in business, that's good for the farmers and us."

Widmer also appreciates having the Center for Dairy Research, which the WMMB helps support, as close as a phone call. "I can call the Center for Dairy Research if I have a problem with my cheese making, and if I want to learn how to make a new cheese."[5]

The WMMB receives high marks from the specialty cheese people, too. "With each passing month and year, the board seems to be doing a better job of promotion," said Dan Carter, CEO of Specialty Cheese Marketing in Mayville.[6]

Why say "cheese" when being photographed? Try saying the word and remaining glum as you consider the absurdity of the act.

Wisconsin Department of Agriculture, Trade, and Consumer Protection

Long active in the promotion of Wisconsin agricultural products, DATCP continues to promote dairy products, especially cheese. One of its outstanding, longtime efforts is the Alice in Dairyland Program.

Alice in Dairyland

The Alice in Dairyland program began in 1948. Many Wisconsin organizations were planning activities for the state's centennial that year, and it was important that organizations related to the dairy industry be well represented. The Wisconsin Department of Agriculture, with deep ties to the dairy industry, wanted to make a special effort. Donald McDowell, who started

---

5. Gloria Hafemeister, "Fourth-graders learn cheese making at Theresa factory," *Wisconsin State Farmer*, May 1996.

6. Kurt Gutknecht, "Cheese manufacturers praise board's efforts," *Wisconsin Agriculturist*, March 1997, 11.

The first Alice in Dairyland, Margaret McGuire, toured the state in 1948 promoting Wisconsin cheese and the Centennial Exposition. Chaperones were Donald and Ardith McDowell. Donald McDowell later became director of the Wisconsin Department of Agriculture.

—From Donald McDowell.

working for the department in 1947 (he later became director), recalled, "We wanted to do something special for the centennial. So we came up with the idea of Alice in Dairyland. It was a way of promoting Wisconsin dairy products, especially Wisconsin cheese. We made a huge replica of the Alice we selected— Margaret McGuire—and had it on the fairgrounds at the State Fair, which went on for a month in 1948."

Those attending the fair in Milwaukee couldn't miss seeing the eleven-foot-tall replica of Alice standing outside the dairy building. Children stood in awe in front of it, and were even more surprised when the doll spoke to them. A young woman was inside. She answered questions and talked about Wisconsin's dairy industry.

McDowell said, "My wife Ardith and I were chaperones for Alice that first year. We traveled throughout the state attending most of the county fairs. We used convertible Chevrolet cars that were donated to us."

"Alice" was so well accepted that the Department of Agriculture decided to continue the program. In 1952-53, Alice became a full-time employee. Her mission was to promote dairy products. Later, the job was expanded to include all Wisconsin agricultural products.

McDowell recalled a special cheese promotion in 1953. "In that year the University of Wisconsin football Badgers played in the Rose Bowl in Pasadena. We saw this as an opportunity to take Wisconsin cheese to California. We couldn't find a pound of Wisconsin cheese in the entire state of California. With Alice in Dairyland and the Rose Bowl, we opened up the West Coast market for Wisconsin."

The statue of Alice in Dairyland was displayed for several years at the State Fair in Milwaukee. Each year the facial features were changed to match those of the current Alice, who is selected annually.

In 1997, the year the Green Bay Packers went to the Super Bowl in New Orleans (and won), the reigning Alice in Dairyland, Holly Meudt, traveled around Wisconsin stamping foam "Cheeseheads" (as well as ties, caps, and other Packer-backer cheddar-wear) with the Department of Agriculture, Trade, and Consumer Protection's official cheese-grading logo.

The Alice in Dairyland program continues, with a young woman selected during June Dairy Month. She works for one year. Currently, applicants for Alice in Dairyland must have four years of training, education, or experience in communication, marketing, agriculture, public relations, or consumer science, or a combination of these. They must be female Wisconsin residents. During her year of service, "Alice" logs the equivalent of two trips around the world, while traveling by car throughout Wisconsin.

Barbara Haslow, the 1958 Alice in Dairyland, accepts an aged cheddar cheese from Ronald Johnson of Mt. Sterling. Haslow appeared on "Queen for a Day" in Hollywood promoting Wisconsin cheese.

—From Wisconsin Department of Agriculture, Trade, and Consumer Protection.

Export Program

Wisconsin is the leading producer of cheese in the nation, making more than twice as much as California, its nearest competitor.

U.S. exports of cheese, yogurt, and ice cream have risen nearly 100 percent from 1990 to 1994—from $86 million to $170 million. Prime export markets are Mexico, Japan, Southeast Asia, Korea, and Latin America.

Wisconsin leads the nation in dairy product exports; the state's products accounted for about twenty-five percent of total U.S. dairy exports in 1994. DATCP assists Wisconsin's firms with their export operations by offering seminars and conferences related to export opportunities. It also helps processors who wish to exhibit at international trade shows, such as the Festival de Alimentos y Bebibas (FAB) trade show in Mexico, the U.S. Food Export Show, and the World Food Show in Moscow. In 1996, DATCP celebrated thirty years of providing international trade assistance to Wisconsin agribusinesses.[7]

7. Information on the Wisconsin Dairy Export Program is from the author's conversation with Karen K. Endres of the Wisconsin Dairy Export Initiative of the Wisconsin Department of Agriculture, Trade, and Consumer Protection.

14 *The Funny Side of Cheese*

When I asked one old cheese maker with more than forty years experience to share something humorous about the cheese business, he said, "Nothing funny about making cheese. It's darn serious business." He meant that, too. He went on to tell me how he often went to work at three in the morning and seldom finished before seven in the evening, seven days a week. He told me about winter days and frozen milk, and hot summer days and sour milk. "Not a darn thing funny about making cheese," he said.

This fellow was an exception, however. Others shared an array of humorous stories that are included throughout this book. It's not only cheese makers who see a funny side to cheese; lots of other people do, too.

Cheeseheads

One of the funniest things to come down the country road is the Cheesehead phenomenon. Who'd ever think that grown people would sit in public wearing a strange triangle-shaped piece of yellow foam with holes in it on their heads? But go to any Green Bay Packer game (Brewer games, too), and there they are—hundreds of them. They look like they just arrived from some strange planet, or perhaps from the moon, because we all know the moon is made of cheese.

Ralph Bruno is the chief honcho for the Foamation Company in Milwaukee, the home of the fast-becoming-famous Cheesehead. Bruno had started working at Schneider Pattern Works in

Milwaukee in 1979 as an apprentice pattern maker. In 1985, while still working at Schneider, he and a co-worker built their own pattern shop in Dousman, not far from Milwaukee. The Dousman operation was initially a moonlight job, but turned into full-time work after a few years.

In April 1987, Bruno fabricated a Cheesehead made of foam. "I got the idea because I'd heard Chicago people were calling us 'cheeseheads.' I felt this was not a bad thing. On the contrary, I felt being a cheesehead was something a Wisconsin resident should be proud of," Bruno said.

If Chicago people were calling Wisconsin folks cheeseheads, Bruno reasoned that maybe wearing a Cheesehead hat could turn a slam into a success. So what kind of cheese should the hat represent? "When I made the hat, I wanted people to recognize it as cheese from a distance. I felt the shape had to be like a wedge, because it would have more visual impact than a slice or a wheel," Bruno said.

University of Wisconsin-Madison band decked out in Cheeseheads.

—From Ralph Bruno.

The next design question he faced was color. "The color had to be a characterized version of cheese so other people would understand what it was. Swiss cheese is white. Cheddar cheese is orange. My idea was a color that did not associate with any one cheese." Bruno came up with yellow.

"The hat still needed more, so I added holes, but the holes are different on a Cheesehead as opposed to real cheese. Again, I wanted to disassociate from Swiss, so the holes on a Cheesehead are not perfect spheres or bubbles, but irregularly shaped and flattened depressions, unlike real cheese. The result of all this was a cheese that does not exist."

Bruno wore his new creation to a Milwaukee Brewers game. "I got mixed reactions," Bruno said. "Some of the people seated near me moved several seats away. Others gathered around asking where I had purchased my hat. The light bulb flickered on, and I spent the remainder of the game thinking about how I was going to build a mold."

The next day Bruno built his mold and figured out how to manufacture it. He asked a polyurethane foam molder to give him a bid for making Cheeseheads, but the tooling cost was too high. Bruno decided to figure out the molding process himself. The early results were good, and he started pounding on doors looking for markets. Sports Service, a vendor at Milwaukee County Stadium, was an early market. Although the profit margin was slim, the publicity and exposure were great.

Sales increased. Bruno added other Cheesehead items, such as baseball caps, neckties, bow ties, cowboy hats, footballs, and clocks. The Foamation Company was created in 1988. At that time, Bruno separated from the partnership in the pattern company to devote more time to Foamation. He moved his new company to the south side of Milwaukee. He added his sister, Kathy Bruno, and his Uncle Joe to the business. Kathy and Joe set up the office and the books.

Up to this time, Bruno had but one Cheesehead mold. He realized he needed more molds to increase production and he needed to develop a process for making a large number of Cheeseheads. Sales warranted more employees and more factory space. Chris Becker was hired as general manager. "When Chris joined Foamation, it allowed me to focus on mold making and production machinery," Bruno said.

By the late 1990s, the company was expanding rapidly. It developed a computer mail order system and an Internet page. Mass mailings were sent all over the country. Foamation also licensed companies to use Cheeseheads for commercial use. Large department stores began carrying the products. Exhibits at the Wisconsin State Fair, Monroe's Cheese Days, and the Warrens

Cheddarhead exhibit at Monroe Cheese Days, 1996.

Cranberry Festival helped increase sales and public awareness.

A great boost for Cheeseheads was their association with the Green Bay Packers football team. The national TV network cameras panned the crowds at Lambeau Field, and wedge-shaped yellow hats with holes in them appeared. Then a light plane crashed in central Wisconsin, and Cheeseheads were in the news, not just sports news but the national news. Frank Emmert of Superior was returning home in his two-seater plane from a trip to Ohio where he had been watching the Green Bay Packers play the Cleveland Browns. When he realized his plane was going to crash, he put on his Cheesehead hat to protect his head. "I could have used a pillow, I could have used my coat, but I grabbed that darn cheese, and I'm glad I did; it really helped to protect my head," said Emmert. Soon the world was hearing about it from Emmert's hospital room in Stevens Point. In a short time, Emmert was face-to-face with Jay Leno on the "Tonight Show," after zooming onto the set in a cart shaped like a wedge of cheese.

After this, nearly everyone seemed to know about Cheeseheads. Most Wisconsin people, but not all, applauded the great publicity the state and the cheese industry were receiving. "Any publicity is good publicity, even if the cheese depicted does not exist," said John Umhoefer, executive director of the Wisconsin Cheese Makers Association, with a smile.[1]

---

1. George Hesselberg, "Even fake cheese is positive advertising," *Wisconsin State Journal*, January 10, 1997.

Then in 1996, it became clear by midseason that the Green Bay Packers were not the Packers of recent years, but were winning. Maybe, just maybe, they would make it to the Super Bowl. They did. A semi truck with a huge supply of foam hats, caps, ties—whatever—for the Wisconsin faithful followed the Packers to New Orleans. A second semi loaded with Cheeseheads stopped for celebrations in St. Louis, Memphis, and New Orleans on the way to the Super Bowl.

Michael Bauman, sports writer for the *Milwaukee Journal Sentinel* wrote this about Cheeseheads. "The larger issue is the running cultural debate. The anti-Cheesehead argument is that if you wear that sort of head gear, people will think that you are a rube, a yokel, a hick, and a hayseed. In fact, people will generalize from wearing that Cheesehead and will believe that everybody from Wisconsin belongs in one or all of those categories."

Bauman went on to write, "The harsh truth is that a lot of people think that anyway. What do they really know about us? Almost nothing. But you could wear the fanciest fedoras and that wouldn't change their minds, either. The Cheesehead thing works only because it turns a term of derision—you'll pardon the expression—on its head."[2]

It is not only at sports events that the foam Cheesehead turns up. The 1996 Democratic Convention in Chicago included some Wisconsin delegates sporting the famous hat. The wearing of the cheese caught the attention of the Smithsonian Institution. Their National Museum of American History wanted a Cheesehead that had been worn at the convention. Harry Rubenstein of the Smithsonian said, "The Cheesehead is just a nice symbol of local pride, local identification. We'd like to have it as a document."

Pat Hawley of Sturgeon Bay, a convention delegate, heard of the request and donated her Cheesehead, complete with Clinton/Gore bumper stickers on the side and a propeller in front. The Cheesehead went to Washington.[3]

In 1996, the Smithsonian added a Cheesehead to its collection.

—From Ralph Bruno.

---

2. Michael Bauman, "Cheeseheads put loyalty head first," *Milwaukee Journal Sentinel*, October 4, 1996.

3. "Cheddar chapeau off to Smithsonian," *Capital Times*, September 28, 1996.

The Cheesehead debate will go on. But no matter how it turns out, Cheeseheads are about Wisconsin. There is a contrary note, however. The Dutch also think they are "cheese-heads," and they, too, make lots of cheese, being a major world exporter. In Dutch, "cheese-head" is another word for the mold in which cheese is made. The story goes that during the Middle Ages, farmers in North Holland used their wooden cheese molds as helmets. It was easy for an invading army to identify the Dutch "cheese-heads."

Cheddarheads

Not to be confused with Cheeseheads, Cheddarheads are cartoon characters created by an organization that has its headquarters in La Crosse. T. J. Peterslie, an artist, started the company in 1986. "It was in response to Illinois visitors coming into the state and poking fun at Wisconsin people," Peterslie said. Rather than toss barbs back, Peterslie developed cartoon characters. They too seem to poke fun at Wisconsin people. "But the cartoons have a deeper message," said Peterslie. "It's about Wisconsin pride."

The Cheddarhead family on its way to Green Bay. Cheddarheads have become popular in Wisconsin and throughout the world, appearing on everything from calendars to T-shirts.

Like the Cheeseheads, the Cheddarheads have a tie to the Green Bay Packers. "When the Cleveland Browns left Ohio, we received many orders for Wisconsin Cheddarhead materials," Peterslie said. "One man said he had never been in the state, but he liked the way the Packers and the Wisconsin people related to each other and he wanted to be a part of it."

After the *Milwaukee Journal* did a feature story on Cheddarheads in 1986, sales took off. "We send out 40,000 catalogs at a time," said Peterslie. "It's almost a cult thing. People photocopy catalogs and send them to each other. Word of mouth is selling our products."

The Cheddarheads' antics appear on shirts, cards, calendars, mugs,

THE CHEDDARHEADS

PACKERS — PKR BKR

EVERYONE ELSE GOES TO FLORIDA AND WE GO TO GREEN BAY!

and cheese labels. The family consists of Ted, Louise, Teddy, Betty, and Cheddarbear. According to the promotional material, "The Cheddarheads live in Polka, Wisconsin, population 12,000. They are stout, good-natured folks who know that beauty is only skin deep…. what is important is that you have a good head on your shoulders [preferably a Cheddarhead]. Their fashion statement is casual and cow-spotted; their humor, a real slice of Wisconsin."

The Cheddarheads: Wisconsin Gothic.

To date, Peterslie has created more than a hundred cartoons, which he believes "have become a symbol for Wisconsinites and created a national Cheddarhead movement." Cheddarhead merchandise has been shipped to every state in the nation and many countries of the world.

Cheddarhead cartoons vary from hilarious to "huh?" A classic portrays two Cheddarheads in a snow-covered car in a snowstorm. The bumper stickers say, "Packers" and "Pack is Back." The license plate reads, "PKR BKR." The caption says, "Everyone else goes to Florida and we go to Green Bay." Then there is the cartoon of the Cheddarhead couple on a Florida beach. She is wearing a bathing suit and is talking on her cell phone. He is on a beach chair, fully dressed in his winter finery, including his snow boots, stocking cap, and long red scarf. The caption: "I'm fine, but he misses Wisconsin."

Another one that nudges the funny bone shows the Cheddarhead family, all with their cheese heads, of course, lined up in front of a photographer. The photographer says, "OK, now…ready…1-2-3, say Wisconsin."

Recently the Cheddarhead company sponsored a photo contest. People were supposed to send in photos wearing Cheddarhead clothing. The idea behind the contest was, "wherever you are, whatever you are doing…if you're wearing one of these shirts, people will recognize that you are proud to be from the Land of the Badger, the State of the Robin, and the Home of the Cheddarheads."

The company received photos from Scotland, Saudi Arabia, Japan, Hawaii, Africa, Russia, Bora Bora, England, the Great Wall of China, and Aztec ruins in Mexico. One was taken during the dismantling of the Berlin Wall. A prizewinning photo came from EMC/SS Jerry Hottinger, who was stationed aboard a nuclear submarine near the North Pole and is shown standing on the ice near the submarine, wearing his Cheddarhead shirt.

The Cheddarhead Company has its main store in downtown La Crosse, across the street from the Civic Center. They have resisted selling their materials through other distributors, though have often been requested to do so.

The Packers and Cheese

The Wisconsin Milk Marketing Board, not to be outdone by all the hoopla over the Packers' success in the 1996-97 season, decided to pair cheese with Packer personalities. Here are some examples:

• Mike Holmgren, coach: blue cheese—great when grilled.
• Reggie White: cheddar—very popular, increasingly complex with age, can come in mammoth packaging, highly prized.
• Brett Favre: Provolone—considered country, intensifies and sharpens with age.

In 1997, the Wisconsin Milk Marketing Board developed a poster featuring Packer quarterback Brett Favre and Wisconsin's prizewinning cheese varieties. The poster was available at retail cheese counters for customers who purchased at least two pounds of Wisconsin cheese.

Say Cheese

Have you ever stood in front of a camera and had the photographer command, "Say cheese?" A rather common occurrence, at least in my experience. But what does the word "cheese" have to do with picture taking? With that question in mind I set out to do some research on the topic. As someone who takes many photos during the course of a year, I regularly have asked people to say

Swiss cheese is best known for its holes, some as large as a quarter. Contrary to popular myth, the holes in Swiss cheese are not formed by mice, an elephant shooting peanuts, or cheese makers patiently putting cheese around the open places. The holes are formed by special bacteria working in the cheese.

cheese. I decided to examine my photos closely to see what happened when a subject said the word "cheese" just before I snapped the shutter.

I also did some in-front-of-the-mirror research, which means I said cheese repeatedly as I watched my facial features.

Here are the results of the research, a real contribution to scientific knowledge because I have not heard of anyone conducting such important inquiry before.

Nine of the ten people I observed opened their mouths when they said "cheese." Eight of them also smiled, and the ninth one smirked, which could be considered a smile without destroying the validity of the research. The tenth one was a distant relative of mine who people believe hasn't smiled since sometime before World War II; saying the word "cheese" just before having her picture taken certainly wasn't going to break such an outstandingly sullen record.

My in-front-of-the-mirror experience, conducted innumerable times until I began to feel like my sour relative, revealed that you cannot say cheese without opening your mouth. With your mouth open and your mind considering what you are doing, the natural thing to do is smile. After all, it is more than a little dumb to have a collection of people all saying cheese at the same time with their mouths hanging open. Might as well smile at the absurdity of the moment.

After this bout of research, I explored the issue a little farther. Through the Internet, I contacted several international linguists. Typical of the replies I received was this one from Deborah D. K. Ruuskanen, of Helsinki, Finland. "In English you say 'cheese' when someone takes your photograph because the pronunciation of the word in English requires you to stretch your lips in a smile. The word 'muikku' in Finnish, for example, is used for the same reason. Nothing basically to do with the meaning of the word, just the position of the mouth to make the long 'ee' vowel sound."

The Cheese League

Football is serious business in the minds of many people, especially its fans. But mentioning "cheese league" brings a smile to even the most ardent football follower, for it means professional teams are conducting summer training camps in the cheese state. The Green Bay Packers have long stayed home for their summer camp. But other teams, especially those who come from places where summer temperatures are torrid, enjoy a respite in a state in which the temperatures are cooler and the cheese is piled high. Summer camps tend to start in mid-July and end in mid-August; not a long time, but a fun one for Wisconsin football lovers.

The Chicago Bears practice on the campus of the University of Wisconsin-Platteville, which is not that many miles from the windy city but a major change in environment. The New Orleans Saints practice in the comfort of the Mississippi River town of La Crosse, on the campus of the University of Wisconsin-La Crosse. The Kansas City Chiefs trek to River Falls for their summer camp, where they practice on the campus of the University of Wisconsin-River Falls. But alas, the Jacksonville Jaguars, who had been coming to Stevens Point for summer camp, opted out of their contract with the University of Wisconsin-Stevens Point in 1996 to stay home. They said that far more fans would turn out to watch them practice in Florida. Hard to figure why that might be with the Packers only a few miles down the road from Stevens Point at Green Bay, practicing at their Oneida Street field just east of Lambeau Field. Some will remember the 1996 Packers season. Packer fans paid $10 a box for Lambeau Field sod that had to be removed after one of the games. That day Packer sod sold even better than Wisconsin cheese.

The Language of Cheese

The word "cheese" has edged its way into our language in several ways. For instance, "the big cheese" refers to the person in charge, the big boss, the main guy. Sometimes the title is given to someone who fancies one of those positions.

I haven't heard this used for a while, but I remember when people said, "It's just cheesy," meaning something is special or a little extraordinary. Sometimes "cheesy" is used to mean the opposite, something cheap or gaudy.

Then there's "cheese it," which, loosely translated, means, get rid of, put it away, shove it—or some other less than polite term.

The *Dictionary of American Regional English* has some additional meanings for cheese. For instance, "cheese" as a verb can mean to apple-polish or play up someone in order to gain some favor.

"Cheese-eater" is sometimes used to mean a cheater or informer. To say someone is "cheesy" sometimes means that the person is "low-grade, worthless, trashy, cheap, stingy." In some cases, someone who appears pale or peaked is described as looking "cheesy." And the dictionary says that a "cheesehead" is "a stupid, awkward person."[4]

Cheese in Other Contexts

We all know that the moon is made of green cheese; at least that is what I was taught as I sat on my daddy's knee while we looked at the moon on clear summer nights.

Some of us are old enough to know that cheese, especially Limburger cheese, was often a part of the dirty tricks played on newlyweds. The stinky stuff was smeared on the car's exhaust system. The young couple drove a few miles, and when the engine warmed, the cheese made itself known. It was usually the young bride who noticed first, wrinkling her nose and perhaps thinking her new husband hadn't taken time to clean out his car. Soon the smell became so unbearable that the couple could not drive on. By this time, the groom had figured out what had happened, and even had a good idea who did it—probably the friend for whom he had done the same thing a year ago. He rolled up his sleeves, grabbed a screwdriver, and scraped off the mess, and the newlyweds drove on—with a lingering smell of Limburger cheese remaining in the car for weeks.

Everyone knows that if you want to catch a mouse in a trap, you bait it with cheese—a favorite treat for those sneaky little critters that at one time or another invade every rural home and most urban ones, as well. A smart mouse learns how to remove the cheese from the trap without snapping it.

Those who enjoy sitting by a slow-moving river on a lazy summer afternoon with fishing pole in hand, know that catfish are often attracted to a gob of smelly cheese fastened to a hook. Smelly cheese is certainly not in the same category as those flashy fishing lures advertised on TV, but if you want to catch a catfish, especially one of those big old channel cats that live on the

---

4. Frederic G. Cassidy (ed.), *The Dictionary of American Regional English* (Cambridge, MA: Belknap Press of Harvard University Press, 1985), 602-603.

bottom, then smelly cheese it is. If after catching such a prize fish, someone asks what you used for bait, the correct strategy is to remain mum on the subject. Those who ask will assume you have used some fancy, expensive artificial bait displayed in sport stores. Let them assume what they will. Cat fishermen know how to keep a secret.

15 *Selected Cheese Factories*

The story of Wisconsin cheese is told in the stories of the state's cheese factories. Here are brief descriptions of a few representatives. Some of these factories are small; a few are large. Several have been in the same family for generations. A few are cooperatives that are owned by the farmers who deliver milk to them. Some of the smaller factories make special cheeses, a practice that enables them to survive despite great odds. Almost all of those described have changed with the times, adding new technology and becoming adept at marketing their products.

Beechwood Cheese Factory

N1598W County A
Town of Scott
Sheboygan County

According to historian Edwin Fisher, Sheboygan County had 120 cheese factories in 1905, which he believes was the peak year. Beechwood Cheese Factory is a good example of a Sheboygan County factory that put down its roots early, has had many owners, and yet succeeds as a family-operated enterprise.

In 1882, John O'Connell bought a farm in the town of Scott. Soon he was operating a cheese factory, and by 1887 he was receiving 1,700 pounds of milk a day.

The factory was sold several times over the years. By 1905, when John Jonssen owned it, the factory had 130 farmer patrons, the largest number of any factory in Sheboygan County.

The Beechwood Cheese Company was formed in 1943, with Ed Conger as cheese maker. In 1944 the Deland Company took over, but by 1948 they were forced to cede ownership to the Citizens Bank of Sheboygan. Norbert Heise, who had been working for the Deland Company, bought the plant in 1956.

Heise made cheddar cheese in mammoths, longhorns, and twins. He also made Colby, brick, muenster, and a special Italian cheese for grating. The Borden Company helped him become what is believed to be the first cheese maker in Wisconsin to make Monterey Jack cheese.

Since 1979, Norbert's son, Mark, and his wife, Kris, have operated the factory. They continue to produce muenster, brick, Monterey Jack, Colby, and cheddar, and they specialize in forty-pound-block Colby Jack and jalapeño-pepper cheese.[1]

Cady Cheese Factory

126 Highway 128
Wilson
St. Croix County

The Cady Cheese Factory is an example of a factory that started small, suffered adversity, and always came back to making cheese, which it does today.

Cady Township, in which the Cady Cheese Factory is located, had a scant 158 acres of wheat, ninety-nine acres of oats, and fifty-one acres of corn in 1876. The population was 329, and there were no dairy plants of any kind. Lumber milling was the prominent form of enterprise.

But after the lumbermen removed the timber, a vast acreage of land became available for other uses. In the early 1900s, farmers—most of them German—bought land in the area. By 1908, a group of them formed a cooperative and built a cheese factory next to what is now Highway 128. Fred Bohren, a Swiss immigrant, was hired as cheese maker, and he began making German brick cheese. In those early days, the farmers hauled their own milk to the cheese factory and they took turns hauling the cheese to Menomonie or Spring Valley for shipping. Sometime later, the

---

1. Fisher, *The Cheese Factories of Sheboygan County.*

cooperative sold the factory to the cheese maker.

In late 1917 or 1918, the cheese factory burned but was immediately rebuilt. A series of owners followed Bohren, and they operated the plant until about 1928. Benjamin Radel operated the plant in 1930. Arnold Imobersteg took over in 1932. Imobersteg made 180-pound wheels of Swiss cheese. Elmer Gesche, a nearby farmer, hauled cheese with his horses, and also hauled wood to the cheese factory in winter. Imobersteg always had a jug of wine sitting on the boiler during cold winter days—for visitors needing to warm up.

In the 1940s, John Erb, his wife, Freida, and their two children ran the factory. They made large quantities of German brick and Swiss cheese. Both Erb and his wife were born in Switzerland. Herman Gruessi and Don Larrieu worked as hired hands in the plant. One notable event was the day when Larrieu was stirring the milk with a long-handled fork and one of the workers dropped his false teeth into the vat. It took some time to find and retrieve them. If they had not found them, the cheese produced that day would have likely provided a new meaning for the phrase "cheese with a bite."

Muenster cheese was developed by European monks during the Middle Ages.

Erb's nephew, Ernest, ran the factory for a year or two. Marvin and Hazel Seeman purchased the cheese factory in April 1955. In 1963, Norman and Deloris Marcott bought the plant. In 1968, the first bulk truck began delivering milk to the plant. In 1978, the plant quit accepting milk delivered in cans. The Marcotts built a retail store and added living quarters above the cheese factory. In 1971, their son took over the operation, buying the factory in 1978.

By 1990, when Ed Pittman was head cheese maker, the factory was producing about four semi-loads of cheese a week and employed between fifty and sixty full- and part-time workers. But then disaster struck. On the night of March 30, 1990, fire destroyed everything but the retail store, the living quarters, and the milk intake room. The 120 farmer patrons could still ship their milk to the plant, where it was stored in silos and then sold. A new, larger, and more modern factory opened in September 1991. Computers operated much of the new equipment. By the mid-1990s, the plant was processing 400,000 pounds of milk a day, five days a week. On July 1, 1993, Cady Cheese stopped picking up milk from its 130 farmer patrons, choosing to purchase its milk from Mid-America Dairymen, Inc.

The Cady Cheese factory is known for its Colby longhorn cheese. It also produces cheddar longhorn, Monterey Jack, and a combination of Colby and Monterey Jack that it calls Gold'n Jack. The newest addition to the product line is a mini-deli longhorn, which is four inches in diameter—the right size for a burger or sandwich. Cady also makes a large variety of flavored cheeses for their cheese store.[2]

Cassel Garden Farmers Cooperative Cheese Company

4531 County S
Marathon
Marathon County

String cheese is really mozzarella cheese sold in one-ounce strands or ropes.

Cassel Garden is an example of a cheese factory cooperative, one of many that operated in Wisconsin. Its history traces back to 1910, when John Seubert, a real estate investor, built a cheese factory. He hired Anton Schuster, a Swiss immigrant, as cheese maker. The plant made Swiss, cheddar, and brick cheese. Several other cheese makers followed before the Cassel Garden Cooperative Cheese Company was organized on April 15, 1921. (The cooperative took its name from the field of wildflowers that grew around the cheese factory building.) John Lensmire became cheese maker and manager for the cooperative. Twenty-seven farmers bought shares, each agreeing to deliver a cord of wood a year to keep the boiler fired. In its first year of operation, the factory produced 138,830 pounds of cheese. Cheese sold for thirteen cents a pound, but dropped to 9.7 cents a pound in 1933, in the midst of the Depression. During those years, farmers received eighty-two cents per hundred pounds for their milk. By 1940 cheese had gone up to fourteen cents a pound, and farmers received $1.23 per hundred pounds for their milk.

Farmers delivered their own milk to the factory, first with horse-drawn wagons and later with pickup trucks. In 1940, the cooperative purchased its first truck to pick up farmers' milk, and in 1967 the plant put bulk trucks on the road. A new plant was constructed in 1952, with another addition built in 1969. Cassel Garden joined with four other cheese manufacturers in 1974 to

---

2. History Project Committee, *Cows, Creameries and Cheese Factories* (Baldwin, WI: St. Croix County Association for Home and Community Education, 1995).

form a marketing cooperative located in Mosinee.

Calvin and John Lensmire, sons of John Lensmire, an earlier cheese maker at the plant, managed the plant for many years and retired in 1995, turning management responsibilities over to Wayne Hall, a longtime assistant. The plant now has about ten full-time employees. In 1996, Lensmire added a new unloading station for trucks and a new boiler.

The Kurtzweil family have been farmer patrons of Cassel Garden for a long time. As Elaine Kurtzweil said, "I've always loved their annual meeting, with lunch and a great time for all. My two children, while they were still young, always looked forward to the giant doughnuts that were served at the co-op meeting."[3]

Cedar Grove Cheese Inc.

Route 1, Box 72
Plain
Sauk County

Cedar Grove is an example of a family-owned cheese factory that has made many changes over the years. The original factory opened in 1900. The existing cheese factory is a one-story white building; the cheese-maker's house is located across the road.

Ferdie Nachreiner bought the factory in 1947. He had begun working there three years earlier. "When I started, there were fourteen cheese factories within five miles," Nachreiner said. "Farmers still were bringing their milk to the factory."

Robert Wills, the current owner, married Nachreiner's daughter and bought the factory from him in 1989. He is a new breed of cheese maker, with a law degree and a graduate degree in economics. Wills finds cheese making far more interesting than university teaching, which he once did.

The plant receives milk from forty farmer patrons, the majority of them farming within ten or fifteen miles of the cheese factory. Cedar Grove takes in daily about 75,000 to 100,000 pounds of milk.

The plant employs about thirty people, a few of them part-time. Five licensed cheese makers oversee operations. They make

---

3. From Marathon County Historical Society and Elaine Kurtzweil.

five basic varieties of cheese: Monterey Jack, Colby, farmer's, cheddar, and Butterkäse. They make reduced-fat versions of several of these and flavored varieties (tomato and basil cheddar are examples), as well.

Cedar Grove also makes organic cheese, receiving milk from seven certified organic farmers from as far away as Plover, about a hundred miles distant. The factory produces about 12,000 pounds of organic cheese a day.

All together, Cedar Grove makes some forty different kinds of cheese.

"We also do custom work for people," Wills said. "We make a reduced-fat, tomato, basil, and garlic cheese for a fellow who then sells it at the farmers' market in Madison. He comes in and helps us make it. We also make some special pepper cheeses for restaurants."

Cheese curd has always been a popular item in the factory's retail store. Wills has expanded the curd market to larger cities, such as Milwaukee and Chicago, and developed an attractive package that competes well with other snack foods. Currently, Cedar Grove produces 20,000 pounds of curd a week. Most of it goes out to the stores the same day it is made. It has also developed flavored curds, such as Cajun, tomato, and basil.

Chalet Cheese Cooperative

N4858 County N
Monroe
Green County

The Chalet Cheese Cooperative is the only cheese factory in the United States that makes Limburger cheese. The Chalet Cheese Cooperative is located in a small, Alpine-style building on the top of a hill overlooking one of Green County's beautiful valleys. Chalet also makes brick and Baby Swiss cheese. Myron Olson is master cheese maker and manager of the cooperative, which has about thirty-five producers supplying milk. The cooperative began with five dairy farmer members in 1885, at a time when Limburger cheese was made by many southern Wisconsin cheese factories. It has operated as a cooperative ever since.

Carol Tourdot, longtime employee of the cooperative, said, "We get about 85,000 to 90,000 pounds of milk a day from our

Chalet Cheese Cooperative, Monroe, Green County, 1996. This is the only cheese factory in the United States that makes Limburger cheese.

farmers. We make about seven vats of Baby Swiss cheese a day, and we make about four or five vats a week of Limburger cheese."

The popularity of Limburger cheese has fluctuated over the years. Tourdot said, "Five years ago the market for Limburger started dwindling. Now it's starting to go the other way. We used to sell a lot of Limburger to Kraft but they decided they didn't want to handle it anymore so other distributors starting taking it. Then we got a lot of exposure through the newspaper. Sales began picking up again since we are the only cheese factory in the United States making Limburger cheese."

Chalet Cheese Cooperative has won many awards for its regular and smoked Baby Swiss and is recognized for top quality and workmanship.

Country Castle®

· SINCE 1885 ·

BABY SWISS

MADE FROM PASTEURIZED MILK, NATURAL-DAIRY PRODUCT SOURCED-CHEESE CULTURE, SALT & ENZYMES.

KEEP REFRIGERATED

WEIGH AT TIME OF SALE

CHALET CHEESE CO-OPERATIVE, DIST., MONROE, WISCONSIN 53566 ©

U.S. CHAMPION

Baby Swiss cheese curing. Chalet Cheese Cooperative, Monroe, 1996.

Frigo Cheese Company

(Part of Stella Foods, with headquarters in Lincolnshire, Illinois)
Lena
Oconto County

Pasquale Frigo circling Asiago cheese with a wooden hoop so that excess whey could drain and the cheese would dry. Frigo Cheese Factory, Lena, c. 1930.

—From Leo Frigo.

The Frigo family made Asiago cheese in Northern Italy, but in 1907, when economic conditions became grim, Pasquale Frigo immigrated to the U.S. He settled first in Lamont, Illinois, where a large number of Italians lived. He tried to make Asiago cheese there, but had little success. He was unhappy with the milk supply, and he wanted colder milk.

Northern Wisconsin seemed to meet Frigo's requirements. He moved to the Coleman area and began making Asiago. A short time later, he moved to Iron Mountain, Michigan, where a large number of Italian immigrants worked in the mines. The region also had plenty of cool air to flow over Frigo's curing cheese

when he opened the windows of his cheese warehouse. Frigo went door-to-door selling his Asiago cheese and met with some success. He moved across the Menominee River to Aurora, Wisconsin, and about 1918 moved to Pound in Marinette County.

When the cheese factory in Pound burned in 1938 or 1939, the family moved to Lena and bought a cheese plant that had gone bankrupt. It had ten 10,000-pound vats—a large factory for that time.

When Pasquale Frigo died in 1956, the factory continued operating, with his brother, Luigi, and five of his sixteen children managing it (including Leo, who later became president). Luigi sold out his share in 1964.

Pizza was becoming popular during this time, and the plant grew rapidly. Frigo began making mozzarella, as well as Asiago and Parmesan. By the late 1960s, Frigo was making provolone, Asiago, Romano, Parmesan, mozzarella, and several other varieties.

In the 1960s, the Frigo Cheese Company operated plants in Carney, Michigan; Big Stone, South Dakota; Florence, Wisconsin; and in Lena. They also ran a packaging operation in Crivitz.

In 1974, an English company bought Frigo Cheese Company. At that time, their annual sales were about $60 million. But as Leo Frigo said, "The Italian cheese industry was growing so fast we couldn't keep up with it."

In 1974, Frigo employed about 400 workers. The Frigo brothers continued working for the new company, with Leo as president of the Frigo Cheese Subsidiary. His brothers retired in 1980 and Leo retired in 1984.

Frigo Cheese Company was sold in the early 1990s, and then it was sold again to a Dutch firm. A holding company, which also owns Stella Foods, now owns the company. Stella operates the Lena plant. The cheese factory building burned January 5, 1996. A year later, the plant was back in production. To celebrate its recovery, the company delivered packages of string cheese—a new product line—to every household in the village of Lena, population six hundred. It continues to make Italian cheese and sells much of it with the Frigo label.[4]

Stella Foods was for sale in 1997.

---

4. Information on Frigo Cheese Company is from the author's conversation with Leo Frigo.

Grande Cheese Company

Dairy Road
Brownsville
Dodge County

Grande Cheese plant, Brownsville, 1997. One of Wisconsin's large cheese makers, employing about 500 people, Grande has cheese-making facilities in Brownsville, Rubicon, and Wyocena, and whey processing facilities in Friendship and Brownsville. Its warehousing and distribution center is located in Waupun.

Wisconsin boasts several large cheese companies. Grande Cheese Company is one, but it is not a company that seeks publicity. As Edward R. Kerr, president and chief executive officer, said, "We keep a quiet profile here at Grande, choosing not to promote the company so much to the public or consumer, focusing instead on helping our distributors and end-users [pizzerias, delis, and fine Italian restaurants all across the country] improve their operation and serve a better product."

Grande's home office and technology center are located in Lomira. It has its cheese-making facilities in Brownsville, Rubicon, and Wyocena; whey-processing facilities in Friendship and Brownsville; and a warehousing and distribution center in Waupun. The company employs about 500 people.

Grande makes mozzarella, Provo-Nello provolone, aged provolone, Romano, and Parmesan cheeses. The Grande Custom Ingredients Group, a part of Grande, strives to provide innovative

whey products for the food-processing industry. New whey products are tested in Grande's laboratories, and become ingredients in such things as ice cream, baby food, dairy dips and spreads, salad dressings, sauces, gravies, and seasonings.

When you travel past farms in southern and central Wisconsin, you are likely to see the attractive green and white Grande sign, indicating the farmer produces milk for Grande. In 1997, more than 850 Wisconsin dairy farmers shipped their Grade A milk to Grande.[5]

Krohn Dairy Products

N2915 Highway 163
Luxemburg
Kewaunee County

Krohn Dairy Products is an example of a cheese factory that has been in the same family for several generations.

In 1892, Krohn Dairy was a small cheddar cheese and butter-making factory. Albert Gruetzmacher built the first building on the site of the present-day factory. He purchased the land for $1,400. Never active himself in cheese making, Gruetzmacher hired others to make the cheese for him. He was a great-great-uncle of the present owners and a pillar of the community. When he died, a local newspaper reporter wrote that he had been "one of the most progressive residents of the area who stood ready at any time to assist…. He was appreciated for his sterling worth."

Charles Krohn, grandfather of the present owners, began working for Gruetzmacher in 1894. When Gruetzmacher died, Krohn leased the factory from Mrs. Gruetzmacher. In 1907, he purchased the plant for $3,300.

Leo Krohn, father of the present owners, was born in 1916. When he graduated from Kewaunee High School in 1934, deep within the Depression, he had two choices: go to college or work

WISCONSIN

DAIRY PRODUCTS

Since 1892

KROHN

Low Moisture
PART SKIM
MOZZARELLA CHEESE

INGREDIENTS: PASTEURIZED MILK, SALT, ENZYMES, CULTURE.
KEEP REFRIGERATED
TO BE WEIGHED AT TIME OF SALE
PRODUCED BY: KROHN DAIRY PRODUCTS
N2915 STATE ROAD 163, LUXEMBURG, WI. 54217
PHONE# (414) 845-2901

---

5. Information on the Grande Cheese Company is from company publication and correspondence with Edward R. Kerr.

Krohn's Dairy, near Luxemburg in Kewaunee County, in 1996. This factory has been making cheese since 1892.

with his father in the cheese factory. Leo chose to work with his father in what was then still a one-vat factory.

Up to this time, farmers would take turns hauling cheese from the factory to cheese houses in Kewaunee, bringing back salt, which is used in the cheese-making process. Krohn Dairy purchased its first truck for hauling cheese in 1937. During the 1930s and 1940s, the factory had twenty farmer patrons who provided about 6,000 to 8,000 pounds of milk per day.

By 1945, the cheese plant was obsolete in many ways. State standards no longer allowed wooden floors or vats. The Krohns wondered whether to build a new building or go out of business, as many small cheese factories were doing. They decided to build a new, modern plant just south of the old factory.

In 1946, Charles Krohn died and left the operation to his son, Leo. That year, Leo purchased a truck to pick up milk from farmer patrons, although most of them continued to haul their milk to the factory themselves.

As small cheese factories closed, Krohn Dairy bought out neighboring plants. Eventually, it acquired ten other plants, which closed. By 1957, the company had expanded to the point where it needed to add a factory room, an assembly room, a warehouse, and a boiler room.

In 1960, Leo Krohn made a major decision. He began making mozzarella. Soon half of the cheese he was producing was mozzarella. At this time, the factory employed five full-time men, three truck drivers, and two women and a man who came in every morning to package cheese.

By 1960, Krohn Dairy had storage facilities that enabled the company to hold milk over for a day, and Sunday shifts were no longer necessary. By 1977, it no longer was accepting milk cans— all of the milk was transported by bulk milk trucks.

Disposal of whey was always a challenge. In the early days, most farmers hauled whey back home for their pigs or spread it on their fields. In the early 1970s, Foremost Dairy picked up Krohn's whey, but then decided to quit. Facing a crisis, several area cheese factories joined together and built their own whey-processing plant. Ground was broken for the whey plant on November 15, 1973.

In May 1971, Leo Krohn suffered a heart attack. He turned over the plant's operation to his son-in-law, Arlie Doell, and his daughter, Jean Krohn Doell, who was then a teacher. Upon graduation from high school, Roger Krohn, Jean's brother, who had been working in the plant since he was a youngster, officially joined the

Mozzarella cheese loaves floating in salt brine. This is an important step in the manufacture of mozzarella and other types of cheese. Krohn Dairy Products, Kewaunee County, 1996.

Jean Krohn Doell, who with her husband and brothers, owns and operates Krohn Dairy Products in Kewaunee County, 1996.

business. Another brother, Carl, also joined the business when he finished his schooling.

The family has continued to make improvements over the years. New 40,000-pound cheese vats were installed in 1982. In 1987, the retail store and the cooler were enlarged, and a suite of offices was added. In 1988, to meet Department of Natural Resources standards, the Krohns built a separate wastewater treatment plant, which handles 30,000 gallons of waste water per day.

In April 1990, Leo Krohn suffered a fatal heart attack in the cheese factory. He had been born in the old factory, and died in the new one.

Today, his children, Roger, Carl, and Jean, and Jean's husband, Arlie, own and operate the plant. They have about 310 farmer patrons, with the number going down. However, the amount of milk coming in is the same or may be even increasing, as farm herds become larger. Milk is hauled to their plant from about a forty-mile radius, from Kewaunee, Door, and Brown counties.

For the most part, Krohn makes mozzarella, plus some provolone and a little cheddar to sell in its retail store. In late 1996, it was shipping about two million pounds of mozzarella cheese a month. The company employs fifty people, including six licensed cheese makers. It owns and operates eight trucks and works with contract haulers who have five more.

Elaborate and expensive equipment is found in modern cheese factories. Krohn Dairy plant, Kewaunee County, 1996.

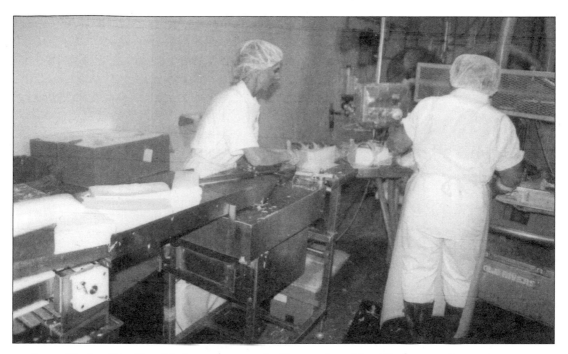

Packaging mozzarella cheese loaves. Krohn Dairy Products, Kewaunee County, 1996.

Jean Krohn Doell said the greatest challenge faced by Krohn Dairy is the competition from mammoth cheese companies, such as the Stella group. "They have a lot of money behind them," she said. But, she added, "We've been able to keep up and compete. What works for us is the personal touch. The farmers know this. They can call and they know who they are speaking to. When we celebrated our centennial a few years ago, we gave plaques to two farms that had been delivering milk to us for a hundred years, as long as we were in business."

Another challenge is the constant tightening of rules and regulations. "Now the Department of Agriculture has decided that you need a license to run a milk pasteurizer," Doell pointed out. "Before, if you had a cheese-making license you could run a pasteurizer. So now we have to license these people. They have to write a test. There are classes in three places in the state, which are limited to 400 people and they are closed, they're full. They are coming up with new rules and regulations constantly."

Another concern that cheese factories such as Krohn Dairy face is the cheese market. "We don't sell all our cheese to one company. If you have companies that go bad, we have to stand the loss. We've had companies that we've done business with for twenty-five years. They pay in thirty days. In thirty days, they may owe us $500,000; even if they get one semi-load a week, they still owe us $200,000 to $300,000. That's a concern [if one of these companies goes bankrupt while they are owing this kind of money]."

Krohn Dairy continues to operate its retail store as a service to the community. Doell recalled the days before they had their retail outlet. "People used to come to the cheese factory. They had to go into the cold cooler for cheese. A line formed on Saturday mornings, and the line actually had to go into the cooler where the cheese was cut. After we put in our store in about 1979, some of the customers said, 'We liked lining up in the cooler.'

"People come from miles around to get our four- and five-year-old cheddar. There's a big demand, with sales increasing," said Doell.[6]

Lynn Dairy, Inc.

W1929 Highway 10
Granton
Clark County

Lynn Dairy has been in the same family since the 1940s. The factory was founded sometime around 1890. By 1896, when Otto Becker operated the plant, sixty area farmers were shipping milk there. The cheese and butter produced were sent to Marshfield.

In 1949, the Schwantes family took over the factory and made many improvements. By the 1950s, they had begun packaging some of their cheese into one-and-a-half-pound chunks with the Lynn label, and were selling them in delis and grocery dairy cases. (Today, packaged cheese accounts for twenty-five to thirty percent of sales. The remaining seventy to seventy-five percent is sold to dealers.)

Lynn Dairy switched to bulk trucks in 1959. It paid a premium to farmers who switched from milk cans to bulk tanks, and even helped farmers finance the installation. It eliminated all milk cans in 1969.

In 1962, the factory purchased its first 7,000-gallon holding tank so that cheese factory workers did not have to work seven

---

6. Information on Krohn Dairy is from *Krohn Dairy Products, Inc. 100th Anniversary, 1992,* and from the author's conversation with Jean Krohn Doell.

Lynn Cheese Factory, Clark County, c. 1896. This was an early version of the factory that operates today on the same site. The cheese factory is the small building in the center of the photo. A sawmill is to the left. Otto Becker operated this factory from 1896 to 1915.

—From Bill Schwantes.

days a week. William Schwantes remembered what it had been like before then. "We always started about 5:30 in the morning. My dad was here then. We'd try to finish by about 3 or 3:30 in the afternoon. Except for the Fourth of July. The Fourth of July was the biggest day in my dad's life. We always told the farmers they could be a half-hour early on the Fourth, so we'd be done with cheese making by noon. We'd play ball down here on the ball diamond; it was just a day for everybody to get together."

Today, the plant receives milk from 236 farmer patrons; they have gained about a hundred patrons since 1990. Five of the seven milk trucks hauling milk to the plant belong to Lynn Dairy. It takes in about 600,000 pounds of milk a day, from which is made about 60,000 pounds of cheese. Cheddar and Colby are specialties, but the factory also makes Monterey Jack and mozzarella.

When the Schwantes took over the cheese factory in 1949, Bill Schwantes' father, Walter, was the only cheese maker. Now there are four licensed cheese makers and about a hundred employees. Lynn Dairy also operates a whey-processing plant.

Bill Schwantes has seen many changes in the cheese industry. He said the quality of milk coming into the plant has improved as a result. "Today milk never gets exposed to air. It is cooled better, too."

A smile spread across Schwantes' face when he related a story

Lynn Dairy, Clark County, 1997. Cheddar and Colby cheeses are its specialties. The dairy makes about 60,000 pounds of cheese a day.

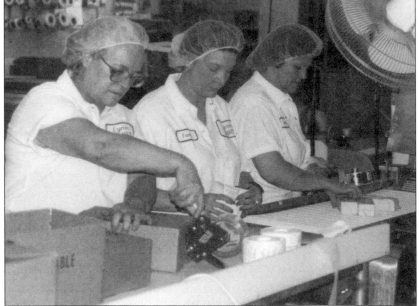

Women packaging and preparing cheese for shipment. Lynn Dairy, Clark County, 1997.

about receiving milk in milk cans. "Many farmers kept minnows for fishing in their cooling tanks. Sometimes when we'd take the covers off the cans and dump the milk a minnow would jump around on the strainer. One time we put water in the milk can after dumping the milk, put the minnow in the can, and took it back to the farmer."

Mt. Sterling Cheese Cooperative

310 Diagonal Street
Mt. Sterling
Crawford County

The Mt. Sterling Cheese Cooperative only makes goat-milk cheese. The factory is owned by the Southwestern Wisconsin Dairy Goat Products Cooperative, a group of about forty goat farmers who have been manufacturing and marketing goat cheese since 1979. Their plant overlooks a valley dotted with dairy barns and surrounded by rolling hills.

Most of the co-op's members live in Wisconsin, but some are in Iowa and Minnesota. They purchased the old Mt. Sterling Cheese Factory in 1983, when demand for quality goat-milk products was increasing rapidly. The co-op's specialty is a cheddar-type cheese, made from raw goat's milk, that is allowed to ripen for at least sixty days. All safety standards are met with the two-month ripening period, and a full flavor results.

Eric Gunderson, cheese maker at the Mt. Sterling cheese factory in Crawford County, packs goat cheese curd into hoops in preparation for pressing, 1996.

The Mt. Sterling Cheese Cooperative in Crawford County, operated by the Southwestern Wisconsin Dairy Goat Products Cooperative, 1996. Goat cheese is one of many specialty cheeses produced in Wisconsin.

Mt. Sterling's cheese has won first place in the Governor's Sweepstakes at the Wisconsin State Fair.

The co-op has two pick-up trucks, which gather milk from goat producers in the region. With dairy goat farmers few and far between, the trucks travel as far as 500 miles a day.

Cheese maker Eric Gunderson said, "Some people must avoid cow's milk and its products. Goat cheese is an alternative for these people. And besides, it is nutritious and tastes good."

Darlene Williams, cheese store manager, has worked in the business for eighteen years and knows cheese making and goat farming. "We have a good mail-order business," she said. "Christmas is when we sell the most cheese by mail." Williams notes that most of Mt. Sterling's cheese is shipped to California.

Prima Käse, Inc.

W6117 County C
Monticello
Green County

Prima Käse is the only cheese factory in the United States that makes Swiss cheese in 180-pound wheels. It is a good example of a small cheese factory that exists among the giants. Located at a crossroads, as so many cheese factories once were, it has as its close neighbors a town hall, an implement dealer, and a feed mill.

Earlier known as the Town Hall Dairy, the factory has been making Swiss cheese since 1948. In 1990, the factory merged with Swiss Valley Farms of Iowa. Randy and Shelly Krahenbuhl purchased the factory from Swiss Valley Farms in 1994 and renamed it Prima Käse.

In the tradition of cheese makers, the Krahenbuhls live above the factory. Both are licensed to make cheese. The factory has windows along one side so a visitor can observe the cheese-making process. In their small retail store, the Krahenbuhls sell a variety of cheeses that the factory produces.

Prima Käse cheese factory, Monticello, 1997. This is one of several small cheese factories in Wisconsin that make specialty cheese, such as Baby Swiss, Wheel Swiss, Gouda, and Edam.

—Photo by Steve Apps.

Shelley Krahenbuhl in the retail store that is part of the Prima Käse cheese factory, Monticello, 1997.

—Photo by Steve Apps.

Besides making 180-pound wheels of Swiss cheese in copper kettles, Prima Käse also makes Asiago, Baby Swiss, Butterkäse, Edam, Havarti, Gouda, and Sweet Swiss. Prima Käse is the creator and sole producer of Sweet Swiss, a type of Swiss cheese that is milder than regular Swiss cheese. In 1996, Prima Käse won the Governor's Sweepstakes Award for its Sweet Swiss and Baby Swiss. That year, Prima Käse's wheel Swiss placed third in the world championship cheese contest sponsored by the Wisconsin Cheese Makers Association.

Randy Krahenbuhl, Prima Käse cheese factory, Monticello, Green County, 1997. This is the only cheese factory in the United States making 180-pound wheels of Swiss cheese.

—Photo by Steve Apps.

Salemville Cheese Cooperative

West 4481 County GG
Cambria
Green Lake County

The Salemville Cheese Cooperative is the only cheese factory in Wisconsin that is owned and operated by Amish. (There is another cheese factory near Cashton that has Amish patrons but is not run by Amish.) The Salemville factory stands in the midst of Amish country. Visit here and you'll likely see Amish children playing nearby and a couple of Amish buggies tied up in back, under the shade of several trees. The cheese factory is one of only two or three establishments that remain in the Salemville community, a place that is no longer even marked on most maps.

Prominently displayed on the wall in the factory's retail store is a shiny plaque that reads:

> Laverne Miller, Cheese Maker
> 1997 U.S. Championship Cheese Contest
> Best of Class 8, Blue, Gorgonzola
> Salemville Cheese Cooperative

The best blue cheese in the nation is made at this little cheese plant. William Schrock, sales manager for the cooperative, said, "We started operating this cheese factory in 1984. We've got forty-four farmers delivering milk to our factory. Thirty-five of them are co-op members. Each sends from a hundred pounds to a thousand pounds of milk each day to the cheese factory."

Milk comes to the plant in ten-gallon cans, making this one of the few cheese factories in the state that still receives milk in cans.

Salemville Cheese Cooperative, Green Lake County, 1997. This cheese factory is operated by Amish families, who make prize-winning blue cheese. It is one of the few cheese factories in the state that accepts milk in ten-gallon cans. Some of the milk is picked up from farmers with horses and a wagon, and the rest is hauled with the truck seen in this photo. The cheese maker and his family live above the factory.

One Amish farmer delivers his milk and that of eight other Amish farmers to the factory with a steel-wheeled wagon pulled by a team of horses. A contract milk hauler from Pardeeville picks up the milk from the rest of the farmers.

"We don't want milk from bulk tanks," says Schrock. "We can't make the kind of cheese we want if the milk is cooled too quickly. Rapid cooling destroys some of the enzymes that give our cheese a special flavor."

About ninety percent of the cheese produced by the Salemville Cheese Cooperative is blue cheese; ten percent is Gorgonzola. When the co-op first began operating, there wasn't much of a market for blue cheese. Then the cheese was put through a drying process that resulted in a powder that could be used for flavoring potato chips and other foods. The market for blue cheese improved. Salemville now sells about seventy-five percent of its cheese to Dan Carter, Inc., a wholesaler who distributes cheese to supermarkets, delis, cheese stores, and restaurants for use in salad bars.

"Dan Carter helped us greatly with our marketing," says Schrock. "The company showed us how to cut our cheese in retail package size and wrap it for the retail market. We do much of the cutting and wrapping right here in the factory. We cut wedges in two- to three-pound sizes, and prepare five-pound bags of blue cheese crumbles."

To meet state rules for sanitation and satisfy the requirements for making quality cheese, electricity in the factory is essential. But the Amish have strict rules against the use of electricity and electrically powered equipment. So that these rules are not violated, the Amish own the business but lease the building.

With one 12,500-pound cheese vat, the factory produces about 1,400 to 1,800 pounds of cheese per day. Milk is not pasteurized but heat-treated to 140 degrees. Heat treatment kills many unwanted organisms, but does not destroy the enzymes and other ingredients in the milk that are necessary for high-quality blue cheese. Because the milk is not pasteurized, the cheese must be cured a minimum of sixty days before it can be sold.

Why does the Amish community run a cheese factory? "We want to preserve the family farm," says Schrock. "Our farmers all milk their cows by hand. If you have a milking machine, you don't need as much labor. A couple of people can do the work of four or five. Milking cows by hand involves the entire family."

16 *Touring Cheese Factories and Museums*

Touring an operating cheese factory offers visitors an opportunity to observe cheese making from the beginning of the process, when milk is pumped into vats, until the finished cheese is packaged and prepared for sale. The sounds, smells, and sights of today's operating cheese factory provide an experience that is truly Wisconsin. Fresh cheese curds are usually available, and many cheese factories operate retail stores in which a variety of cheeses may be purchased, after some tasting.

Cheese factory tours are available throughout Wisconsin: from Barron County in the northwest to Kewaunee County in the northeast; from Grant County in the southwest, through Marathon County in the north-central area, and down, of course, to Green County, in the south. In all, visitors may tour cheese factories in 39 Wisconsin counties.

For those interested in touring an operating cheese factory, two publications provide listings and directions:

Wisconsin Event and Recreation Guide. This free publication lists cheese factories throughout the state that offer tours of their plant. Wisconsin Department of Tourism, 201 W. Washington Avenue, Madison, WI 53703; (800) 372-2737.

Fresh Wisconsin Cheese: From Factory to You. A free county-by-county guide listing factories that feature tours, observation windows, retail outlets, and mail-order operations. Wisconsin

Department of Agriculture, Trade, and Consumer Protection, Marketing Division, P.O. Box 8911, Madison, WI 53708-8911; (608) 224-5111.

Bodenstab Cheese Factory Museum

Now located in the Sheboygan County Historical Museum complex in Sheboygan, the Julius Bodenstab Cheese factory was originally found on Highway A on the western edge of Howard's Grove. Evidence suggests it was built in 1868. The factory closed in the mid-or late 1890s and was used for other purposes over the years.

To many people, the building looks like a typical Wisconsin farmhouse with a two-story section and a one-story room jutting out from the side, with an open porch. The porch was used for receiving milk. The one-story section, which has brick walls, housed the cheese vat. Whey from the vat was drained to an outside whey tank. The two-story section, which has a double layer of lath and plaster, housed the cheese press and provided storage room for materials and cheese.

Today the museum houses a turn-of-the-century cheese vat constructed of wood and lined with tin, various tools used for cutting curd, a Babcock Milk Tester, cheese presses used for removing whey from cheese, and wooden cheese boxes of various sizes and shapes.

The museum is located at 3110 Erie Avenue, Sheboygan. Hours are 10 a.m. to 5 p.m. Tuesday through Saturday, and 1 to 5 p.m. Sunday, April 1-November 1; (920) 458-1103.

Bodenstab Cheese Factory, Sheboygan County Historical Museum in Sheboygan, 1996. Built c. 1868, the factory closed in the mid- to late 1890s and was moved to the museum grounds in 1988. It contains much of the equipment used in cheese factories of the late 1800s.

Heritage Hill State Park

Heritage Hill is a 48-acre living-history museum in Green Bay that consists of several historic buildings, including a cheese factory. The cheese factory was moved from the small community of Ryan in Kewaunee County, where it operated until 1944. The building was donated to Heritage Hill in 1990.

The original factory was built in 1894 of box lumber with a board and batten siding. Interior walls with horizontal tongue and groove boards were added, probably in 1902. A boiler room and steam engine were added in 1905, and the cheese-making room was expanded that year.

The factory replicates cheese making in 1904 with appropriate equipment for that time, including a cheese vat, press, curd knives, cheese boxes, hoops, and assorted tools used for handling cheese curd.

Heritage Hill Museum is located at 2640 South Webster, Green Bay. Hours are 10 a.m. to 4:30 p.m., Tuesday through Saturday, and noon to 4:30 p.m. Sunday, Memorial Day-Labor Day; (920) 448-5150.

The former Clyde Cheese Factory in Kewaunee County is now part of Heritage Hill State Park in Green Bay. It is interpreted as a 1904 cheese factory.

—From Lee Somerville.

Heritage Park Museum

The cheese-making exhibit at this museum in Shawano displays all the equipment needed for making cheese during the early 1900s with the exception of a large cheese vat and cheese press. Tour guides describe the various steps for making cheddar cheese, and explain how farmers were paid for their milk using the Babcock Milk Test for butterfat. The exhibit also includes information about the various dairy breeds.

Heritage Park Museum is located on North Franklin Street at Wolf River Road in Shawano. It is open 1:30 to 4:30 p.m., Wednesday, Saturday and Sunday, June-September; (715) 526-3536.

Historic Cheesemaking Center, Monroe, 1996. Established in 1995 in the former railroad depot, this museum has become a repository of cheese-making research materials for southern and southwestern Wisconsin.

Historic Cheesemaking Center

The Historic Cheesemaking Center in Monroe is a rich resource for anyone interested in learning more about cheese making in Wisconsin, especially Swiss and Limburger cheese. The center is located in a century-old renovated railroad depot—a fitting site considering that millions of tons of area cheese were shipped from it.

Here, visitors learn about the early cheese-making process, from the time the milk entered a cheese factory to when the cheese

Courtney Ott, 1997 Alice in Dairyland, with John Bussman, cheese maker and president of the Historic Cheese-making Center in Monroe. Bussman is dressed in his Swiss costume.

—From John Bussman.

was stacked on the shelves for aging. Enlarged historic photographs from area cheese plants help to make the cheese-making story complete. The photos show cheese makers cutting curd and lifting cheese from copper kettles, and illustrate Swiss cheese wheels aging in factory cellars.

A map on one wall of the center shows the location of all the cheese factories that ever existed in the Monroe area. The center also includes a library in which photographs, video and audio tapes, books, newspaper articles, and other artifacts are available for use by researchers.

Cheese maker John Bussman, who is president of the center, calls it "a shrine to the dairy industry." The center opened in 1995, with the cooperative efforts of Historic Monroe and the Historic Cheesemaking Center. (The Historic Cheesemaking Center shares space with Historic Monroe.) Other groups involved were the Tri-County Trails Commission, Foreign-Type Cheese Makers Association, Wisconsin Swiss and Limburger Cheese Producers Association, and the Green County Tourism Committee. Volunteers donated 6,000 hours to move the old depot, renovate it, and create the exhibits. Local cheese makers and their families have given hundreds of artifacts—historic equipment, photographs, clothing—to the center, knowing that by doing so they would be preserving a long and colorful history.

The Historic Cheesemaking Center is located at Highway 69 and 21st Street, Monroe. Hours are 10 a.m. to 4 p.m., Thursday through Sunday, May 1-October 31, and on Saturday and Sunday only, November 1-April 30; (608) 325-7648.

Kim Tschudy with a Swiss cheese kettle at the Swiss Historical Village, New Glarus, 1996.

Swiss Historical Village

Consisting of twelve buildings, the Swiss Historical Village in New Glarus depicts life in a small town a hundred years ago. One building houses a cheese factory in which Swiss cheese is made during the Heidi festival in June and Labor Day weekend. The exhibit includes 100-year-old cheese-making equipment, including a copper kettle for heating milk that swings over an open fire. There are also examples of "Swiss harps," tools used for cutting the cheese curd.

Swiss Historical Village is located on Seventh Avenue in New Glarus. Hours are 9 a.m. to 5 p.m., May 1-October 31; (608) 527-2317.

Stonefield Historic Site

Everyone knows the moon is made of green cheese.

Near the turn of the century, Grant County had about twenty cheese factories. To commemorate the cheese industry in that area, a replica of a typical cheese factory was constructed at the Stonefield Historic Site near Cassville, which is owned and operated by the State Historical Society of Wisconsin. The cheese factory was constructed as an 1890 factory, complete with cheese vats, presses, curd knives, and a Babcock Milk Tester. It is sponsored by the Wisconsin Cheese Makers Association, the Village of Cassville, and Grant County.

Stonefield Historic Site is located on County VV near Cassville. Hours are 10 a.m. to 4 p.m. daily during May, June, September, and October, and 10 a.m. to 5 p.m. during July and August; (608) 725-5210.

References

Books

Allen, Terese. *Wisconsin Food Festivals*. Amherst, WI: Amherst Press, 1995.

Apps, Jerry. *Barns of Wisconsin*. Madison, WI: Wisconsin Trails, 1995.

Apps, Jerry. *Rural Wisdom*. Amherst, WI: Amherst Press, 1997.

Apps, Jerry. *The Wisconsin Traveler's Companion*. Madison, WI: Wisconsin Trails, 1997.

Athens, Wisconsin, 1890-1990. Wausau, WI: Marathon County Historical Society, 1990.

Buchen, Gustave William. *Historic Sheboygan County*. Sheboygan, WI: Sheboygan County Historical Society, 1944.

Fisher, Edwin L. *The Cheese Factories of Sheboygan County*. Sheboygan, WI: Sheboygan County Historical Society, 1992.

Glover, W. H. *Farm and College: The College of Agriculture of the University of Wisconsin, A History*. Madison, WI: University of Wisconsin Press, 1952.

Hamilton, E. C. *The Story of Monroe*. Monroe, WI: Monroe Public Schools, 1976.

History Project Committee. *Cows, Creameries and Cheese Factories*. Baldwin, WI: St. Croix County Association for Home and Community Education, 1995.

Krohn Dairy Products, Inc. 100th Anniversary, Luxemburg, WI: Krohn Dairy Products, 1992.

Lampard, Eric E. *The Rise of the Dairy Industry in Wisconsin: A Study in Agricultural Change 1820-1920.* Madison, WI: State Historical Society of Wisconsin, 1963.

McMurry, Sally. *Transforming Rural Life: Dairying Families and Agricultural Change, 1820-1885.* Baltimore, MD: Johns Hopkins Press, 1995.

Nesbit, Robert C. *Wisconsin, A History.* Madison, WI: University of Wisconsin Press, 1973.

Odell, Emory A. *Swiss Cheese Industry.* Monroe, WI: Monroe Evening Times, 1936.

Osman, Loren H. *W. D. Hoard: A Man For His Time.* Fort Atkinson, WI: W. D. Hoard and Sons Company, 1985.

Peters, Norman. *Early Cheese Making in Wisconsin.* Fond du Lac, WI, 1989.

Pictorial County Atlas: Green County, Wisconsin. Chicago: The Loree Co., 1954.

Rhine Center Cheese Factory, Sheboygan County, c. 1936. The original factory was built in 1879. The fieldstone factory was built in 1904.

—From Sheboygan County Historical Research Center.

Sanders, George P. *Cheese Varieties and Descriptions*. U. S. Department of Agriculture, Agricultural Handbook No. 54. Washington, D.C., 1953.

Schafer, Joseph. *A History of Agriculture in Wisconsin*. Madison, WI: State Historical Society of Wisconsin, 1922.

Schlebecker., John T. *A History of American Dairying*. Chicago, IL: Rand McNally, 1967.

Smith, Alice E. *The History of Wisconsin: Volume 1, From Exploration to Statehood*. Madison, WI: State Historical Society of Wisconsin, 1973.

Stamm, Eunice R. *The History of Cheese Making in New York State*. Endicott, NY: LeWis Group, 1991.

Stokdyk, A. "Cooperative Marketing by Farmers." In *Farmers in a Changing World: 1940 Yearbook of Agriculture*. Washington, D.C.: U.S. Department of Agriculture, 1940.

Wisconsin Cheesecyclopedia. Madison, WI: Wisconsin Milk Marketing Board, 1995.

Articles, Periodicals, and Booklets

Bauman, Michael. "Cheeseheads put loyalty head first." *Milwaukee Journal Sentinel*, October 4, 1996.

"Cheddar chapeau off to Smithsonian." *Capital Times*, September 28, 1996.

"Cheese Days." *Monroe Times*, September 21, 1996.

"Convention of the Dairymen of Wisconsin." *Jefferson County Union*, February 23, 1872.

"Foremost Farms changing the way it does business." *Wisconsin State Journal*, December 31, 1995.

Gadsby, Patricia. "Light Elements: Why Mosquitoes Suck." *Discover*, August 1997.

Glaze, A. T. "Cheese Factories and Grangers." In *History of Business: In the City and County of Fond du Lac From Early Times to the Present.* Fond du Lac, WI: P. Haber Printing Co, 1905.

Hafemeister, Gloria. "Cheesemaker recalls the rich tradition of his family." *Watertown Daily Times*, April 6, 1996.

Hafemeister, Gloria. "Fourth-graders learn cheese making in Theresa factory." *Wisconsin State Farmer*, May 1996.

Hesselberg, George. "Even fake cheese is positive advertising." *Wisconsin State Journal*, January 10, 1997.

I've Always Wondered About That: A collection of WMMB statements, positions and results, 1994-95 Edition, Madison, WI: Wisconsin Milk Marketing Board, Madison, 1995.

McNair, Joel. "Smaller Cheese Factories Holding Their Own." *Agri-View*, July 24, 1997.

"New Uses for Dairy Products Not So Whey-Out." *Agri-View*, May 23-24, 1996.

"Oak Grove Cheese concentrates on specialty products." *The Country Today*, November 6, 1996.

"Pizza Propels Cheese Consumption Climb." *Agri-View*, May 23-24, 1996.

Roth, Nate. *An Old Cheese Maker's Life*. Monroe, WI: Historic Cheesemaking Center, Monroe (no date).

Somerville, Lee. "Heritage Hill Interpretive Information: The Cheese Factory." Green Bay, WI: Heritage Hill Museum, 1994.

West Bovina Cheese Factory (F. A. Henke, cheese maker), Shiocton, c. 1920.

—From Wisconsin Cheese Makers Association.

Tschudy, Millard. *New Glarus, Wisconsin: Mirror of Switzerland, 1845-1995.* New Glarus, WI, 1995.

Weinschenk, Peter. "New light on Colby Cheese history." *Colby Cheese Centennial Souvenir Edition, Colby Chronicle*, July 12, 1983.

Reports

Adams, H. C. *Biennial Report of the Dairy and Food Commissioner of Wisconsin, 1895-1896.* Madison, WI: Office of the Dairy and Food Commissioner, 1896.

Annual Report of the Dairy and Food Commissioner. Madison, WI: Office of the Dairy and Food Commissioner, 1892.

Babcock, Stephen M. "A New Method for the Estimation of Fat in Milk, Especially Adapted to Creameries and Cheese Factories." In *Seventh Annual Report of the Agricultural Experiment Station.* Madison, WI: University of Wisconsin, 1890.

*Fairview
Cheese Factory
(A. Jorgenson,
cheese maker),
Spring Green,
c. 1920.*

*—From Wisconsin Cheese
Makers Association.*

Babcock, Stephen M., E. H. Farrington, and E. B. Hart. *Methods of Paying For Milk At Cheese Factories*. University of Wisconsin Agricultural Experiment Station, Bulletin No. 197. Madison, WI, July 1910.

Babcock, Stephen M., and H. L. Russell. *The Cheese Industry: Its Development and Possibilities in Wisconsin*. University of Wisconsin Agricultural Experiment Station, Research Bulletin No. 60. Madison, WI, May 1897.

Bakken, Henry H. *American Cheese Factories in Wisconsin*. University of Wisconsin Agricultural Experiment Station, Research Bulletin No. 100, Madison, WI, August 1930.

Cheesemaking in Wisconsin: A Short History. Madison, WI: Marschall Dairy Laboratory, 1924.

Emery, J. Q. *Biennial Report of the Dairy and Food Commissioner*. Madison, WI: Office of the Dairy and Food Commissioner, 1906.

Farrington, E. H., and G. H. Benkendorf. *Organization and Construction of Creameries and Cheese Factories*. University of Wisconsin Agricultural Experiment Station, Research Bulletin No. 244, Madison, WI, 1915.

Henry, W. A. "The Wisconsin Dairy School and Its Work." *Biennial Report of the Dairy and Food Commissioner of Wisconsin for 1899-1900.* Madison, WI: Office of the Dairy and Food Commissioner, 1901.

King, F. H. *Construction of Cheese Curing Rooms For Maintaining Temperatures of 58 degrees to 68 degrees.* University of Wisconsin Agricultural Experiment Station, Research Bulletin No. 70. Madison, WI, January 1899.

Kremer, C. J. *Biennial Report of the Dairy and Food Commissioner of Wisconsin.* Madison, WI: Office of the Dairy and Food Commissioner, 1928.

McKinnon, M. "Response." *Transactions of the Wisconsin Cheese Makers Association.* Madison, WI, 1905.

"Number of Licensed Dairy Plants in Wisconsin, 1895-1942." Wisconsin Crop Reporting Service, Dairy Statistics Bulletin 200, Supplement No. 1. Madison, WI: 1942.

Pickett, J. G. "Pioneer Dairying in Wisconsin." In *Sixth Annual Report of the Wisconsin Dairymen's Association,* edited by D. W. Curtis. Madison, WI: Wisconsin Dairymen's Association, 1878.

"Production by States of All Manufactured Dairy Products, 1940." Washington, D.C.: U.S. Department of Agriculture Bureau of Agricultural Economics, June 1942.

"Revisions in the Production of Creamery Butter, Cheese, and Ice Cream by States, 1910-1939." Washington, D.C.: U.S. Department of Agriculture Agricultural Marketing Service, December 1953.

Russell, H. L. "Dairy Industry in Wisconsin." University of Wisconsin Agricultural Experiment Station, Research Bulletin No. 88. Madison, WI, September 1901.

Schultz, L. H. "Contributions of the Wisconsin Experiment Station to Animal Agriculture." In *One Hundred Years of Research.* University of Wisconsin Agricultural Experiment Station, Madison, WI, March 24, 1983.

"Specialty Cheese Production: Wisconsin, 1993-1994." In *Wisconsin 1995 Dairy Facts.* Madison, WI: Department of Agriculture, Trade, and Consumer Protection, 1995.

Third Annual Report of the Wisconsin Dairymen's Association. Fort Atkinson, WI: W. B. Hoard, printer, 1875.

Thom, H. C. *Wisconsin State Dairy and Food Commissioner Reports, 1890.* Madison, WI: Office of the Dairy and Food Commissioner, 1890.

Wisconsin Cheese Makers Association. *Transactions: Thirteenth Annual Meeting.* Madison, WI, 1905.

Wisconsin Cheese Makers Association. *Fifteenth Annual Meeting.* Milwaukee, WI, 1907.

Wisconsin 1996 Dairy Facts. Madison, WI: Wisconsin Agricultural Statistics Service, 1996.

Videotapes

Videos of cheese makers, milk haulers, and cheese dealers. Monroe, WI: Historic Cheesemaking Center. The center has systematically videotaped people who had a connection to cheese making in southern Wisconsin. Tapes are available for viewing at the center.

Index

Other Books By Jerry Apps

The Land Still Lives

Cabin in the Country

Village of Roses

Barns of Wisconsin

Mills of Wisconsin and the Midwest

Skiing into Wisconsin

One-Room Country Schools

Rural Wisdom

The Wisconsin Traveler's Companion

To order

Cheese
The Making of a Wisconsin Tradition

Rural Wisdom
Time-Honored Values of the Midwest
or
One-Room Country Schools:
History and Recollections from Wisconsin

or for a free catalog of other Amherst Press Books-To-Go titles,
call toll free 1-800-333-8122.

Amherst Press
318 N Main Street
PO Box 296
Amherst, Wisconsin 54406